Establishing a
Token Economy
in the Classroom

The Charles E. Merrill Series on
Behavioral Techniques in the Classroom

Thomas M. Stephens, Consulting Editor

Establishing a Token Economy in the Classroom

WILLIAM C. STAINBACK
Virginia State College

SUSAN B. STAINBACK
University of Virginia

JAMES S. PAYNE
University of Virginia

RUTH A. PAYNE
Albemarle School System

CHARLES E. MERRILL PUBLISHING COMPANY
A Bell & Howell Company
Columbus, Ohio

to Dr. William R. Carriker

Published by
Charles E. Merrill Publishing Company
A Bell & Howell Company
Columbus, Ohio 43216

International Standard Book Number: 0-675-09032-6

Library of Congress Catalog Card Number: 72-93476

Printed in the United States of America

1 2 3 4 5 6 7 8 — 78 77 76 75 74 73

FOREWORD

The Merrill Series on Behavioral Techniques in the Classroom has as its major objective *to improve academic and social instruction*. By using textbooks that focus on systematic applications of behavioral technology in school settings, future practitioners will be better equipped to ssist students in at least three ways. Behavioral techniques, when applied by trained personnel, accelerate learning; they decelerate undesirable responses; and they help maintain learned responses.

Social and academic skills and attitudes are typically acquired more rapidly through behavior modification approaches than when instruction occurs in more conventional ways. The specificity of instructional objectives, the analysis of functioning prior to instruction, the careful application of instructional strategies, and the incentives for responding all contribute to rapid learning and efficient teaching.

Maladaptive, inappropriate, and incorrect responses are modified and reduced in frequency of occurrences. A combination of deliberate activities by teachers results in a reduction of undesirable responses.

Whenever possible, incorrect behavior is not reinforced. Also, conditions are arranged in such ways as to reduce the chances of wrong emissions. And as more time is spent in correct responding, less time is available for undesired behavior.

Behavioral approaches can be effective in helping to maintain past learnings. The functional ways in which learning occurs in directive teaching encourage the use of such learning which contributes to maintenance of the responses. Although the area of maintaining behavior has not been demonstrated as well as initial learning through behavioral approaches, the focus on observable responses seemingly facilitates learning and performance across time intervals.

Each text in this series is devoted to a particular aspect of schooling and/or behavioral methodology. In this text, procedures are described for developing and implementing a token economy in elementary and secondary classrooms.

Contingency contracting, of which token economy is a subclass, is an arrangement of conditions that elicit desired behavior. Contracts, usually in verbal form, are established with the students. Typically, the students are informed that following certain behaviors rewards will follow. In order to extend the responses, tokens are sometimes issued. Thus, as the authors have correctly noted, token economy is akin to our monetary system.

The authors have made an important contribution to teacher training and, indirectly, to improving instruction of children and youth. In this book, you will find sound advice, examples, and encouragement for using token economy systems in classrooms. For too long, token systems were mistakenly believed by many to be useful only when applied to reluctant learners and seriously disturbed individuals. Recently it has become increasingly clear that contingencies are extremely effective when applied to any individual.

This book will hold your interest. It will give you fresh ideas about classroom teaching, and it provides hope for a more scientific approach to teaching. It can not change your behavior, but it will get you started towards that objective.

Thomas M. Stephens
Consulting Editor

PREFACE

It is without question that communication is very important to the educational process. One of us had the importance of communication brought vividly to his attention several years ago when he was struggling to complete his doctoral dissertation. One of the members of the committee that was charged with guiding him through to the completion of the dissertation, kept saying, "You had better get Popham." The response to this was, "I will! Man, you better believe I'll get poppin'." At this crucial time, there was a breakdown in communication. The committee member was recommending a statistical textbook authored by W. James Popham, while the writer through he meant he should start working faster and harder. The result was that he later got both poppin' and Popham.

Very few educators would argue about the importance of communication; we feel that a token economy provides a clear, precise, and easily understood system of communication. An analogy can be drawn between a token economy and the monetary reward system which operates primarily in adult life in this country. Just as the meaning of money is understood by almost every adult, the meaning of tokens is understood by nearly every child who becomes a participant in a token economy. Therefore, we like to think of a token system as a means of enhancing teacher-student communication in the classroom.

Establishing a Token Economy in the Classroom was written primarily for the novice in token reinforcement. For this reason, chapters 3 and 4 give detailed suggestions, recommendations, and explanations regarding what is involved in the proper implementation of a token program. Chapters 1, 2, 5, 6, 7, 8, and 9 provide essential supplementary information that is needed to give chapters 3 and 4 meaning within the context of education in general and specifically behavior modification.

This book is intended for introductory courses to behavior modification and as a resource book for methods courses for elementary, secondary, and special education teachers. It is also suitable reading for any teacher, supervisor, or principal of elementary or secondary education who may be interested in the practical aspects involved in the establishment of a token economy.

The authors wish to express their appreciation to the many students at the University of Virginia and Virginia State College who offered constructive suggestions throughout the preparation of this book. Sincere appreciation is extended to Drs. Romaine Brown, William Carriker, and Donald M. Medley for their encouragement and support. We would also like to thank Miss Jean Yen for searching the education index for some of the references included.

CONTENTS

1 Changing Children for Better or Worse, 1
2 Using the Basic Principles of
   Behavior Modification, 7
3 Answers to Some Basic Questions, 17
4 Step-by-Step Procedure, 35
5 Procedures for Teaching Teachers, 49
6 Limitations of Behavior Modification:
   Fact or Fallacy? 57
7 Articles, Books and Films, 65
8 A Token Economy Implemented with Educable
   Mentally Retarded Pupils, 101
9 Review and Last-Minute Advice, 113

Establishing a Token Economy in the Classroom

1

Changing
Children for
Better or Worse

The basic purpose of this book is to explain how to establish a token system in such detail that any teacher, after studying the book, will have sufficient information to develop and successfully execute a token system in his classroom. The authors reviewed most, if not all, published materials pertaining to token systems and implemented several token systems, both highly successful and moderately successful, in public schools. We then concluded that a token system could be used as an effective tool in most children's educations. Our conclusion led to the development of *Establishing a Token Economy in the Classroom.*

This is not to say that all children should experience and/or be exposed to a token system; however, every teacher, whether elementary, secondary, or special, should be at least exposed to what a token system can do, has done, and will do for certain children. Every teacher-training institution should provide at least enough information pertaining to token systems to enable a professionally trained person to discuss the problems and values of such a system intelligently, and should also provide an opportunity to actually participate in such a system.

Before getting into the nitty-gritty of token system implementation, it may be appropriate and worthwhile to share our beliefs pertaining to token systems as well as a little of our personal educational philosophy.

We would like to clarify that a token system is not a cure-all. The establishment of a token system in a classroom will not *make* kids learn, it will not make children smarter, nor will it develop better personalities in teachers. It might settle the students down so that the teacher can get their attention, it might stimulate students to learn certain academic concepts, or it might help teachers to communicate with children; but it won't produce miracles, in spite of what some behavioral specialists have claimed.

Since all children do not develop at the same rate nor in the same manner and since the basic goal of education is to help each child achieve his maximum potential, then probably the best way to achieve this educational goal under the present circumstances is through individualized instruction. If individualized instruction is necessary, or at least desirable in an educational setting, then a means of communication needs to be established that is as versatile and varied as individuals. Such a system exists with adults. It is commonly known as "money." Some people say money talks; we would like to add that it talks in a lot of different ways at different levels and in different languages. An individualized means of communication in a classroom setting could be money or, equally as effective, tokens exchangeable for activities, objects, free time, etc. Some kids don't get excited by smiles, thank yous, gold stars, Friday afternoon cupcakes, or expressions of love. However, there is not a kid alive that isn't interested in something. The task of an effective teacher is to find the key that motivates *each* child in his room and then use it to enhance the child's intellectual, social, and psychological growth.

Most children are good average kids. They either like to please adults or are afraid of adults, and therefore do their school work. However, as we pursue excellence in our teaching practices, we are no longer satisfied to teach only to the average child. We would prefer *all* children learn and grow. Helping average children to learn is a difficult task, to say the least; but helping children who do not learn through traditional methods is near impossible unless communication between child and teacher is so well developed that a clear and consistent understanding is conveyed throughout the school day. One system — and a very effective system at that — which might help a teacher in his communication process is a token system. A teacher can use a token system as a means of communicating to each and every child in his room on matters he feels are important, regardless of the child's intellectual, social, or psychological stage of development. All he has to do is to get across that when a kid gets a token, he's done "good." This communication is achieved similarly when piece-rate workers are told that they are doing a good job; yet the teacher's role is far more important, complex, and gratifying than the industrial dispenser of financial coins.

Teachers are potent forces in the education of a child. Most, if not all, children's behaviors are learned; and they are learned, in most instances, in the presence of adults. Since a child spends a great deal of his childhood in school, teachers actually help mold children's thoughts, concepts, and behaviors. Teachers can build a child or tear a child down. The more powerful a teacher, the greater the impact on the child. If education is important, then adults assigned to educate children are important. We do not say children can't learn on their own, nor do we say children shouldn't learn on their own. But the greatest source of learning comes through interaction with and between individuals. Interaction connotates communication; and if teachers can communicate, kids learn whether they like it or not. And those teachers who communicate the best seem to be liked the most.

The purpose of any educational endeavor is to change the learner in some way. The child who is exposed to a first grade teacher should be different at the end of first grade than he was at the beginning. The worst thing that could happen to a teacher would be to expose himself, his talents, and his skills to a child and have the child remain unaffected.

Basically educators have evolved from a field of conservatives. Instead of trying to change kids, to excite them, they have had a strong fear of the possibility of hurting the children to the extent that they have been content to maintain the status quo. The dominance of the stronger desire not to hurt anybody over the desire to stimulate has led us into an era of ineffective education. Effective education changes kids; effective teachers change kids.

Now for the kicker — effective communication systems change kids, but the ability to change *does not necessarily connotate change for the good.* Thus, education must strive to be effective, yet be effective in a positive way; that is, have *positive* effects on children. This directional influence of education on children lies, to a large extent, in the hands of the teacher, not the child, parent, school system, or the President of the United States. It lies in the hands of the teacher; therefore, teachers must use every device known to man to help children learn. Most certainly, we must employ teachers who do not wish to hurt children, but we must also terminate teachers who are unable to demonstrate skill in getting kids interested. A teacher who uses a token system is using a powerful tool, and he most certainly can use this tool to do harm as well as good. Therefore, it is imperative that the teacher consider the welfare of his children at all times. No child can participate in a well executed token system and remain unchanged and unchallenged.

The teacher and the child he teaches are at the heart of the educational process whether we like it or not. We wish we could say the child *is* the heart of the educational process, but we have seen too many children die educationally to believe they are the sole heart of the process. We would rather believe children and teachers *share* both success and failure in the education arena than see one championing the other. For example, a seven-year-old child asked an adult to watch her ride her bike. The adult asked, "Why do you want me to watch?" and the child said, "So you can tell me when I do good and when I do gooder." Some people would say, "Yes, you see I told you, the child is at the center of learning"; but we would like to stress that when the adult informed the child that he couldn't watch her at that particular moment, the child decided not to ride. When the adult finished the task at hand fifteen minutes later and told the child he could watch now, the child rode and rode and rode until the adult got tired of watching.

Good teachers want kids to be able to make decisions on their own and to be independent. Therefore, good effective teachers use tools and techniques to assist children in attaining this goal. We believe education and life are too important and too exciting to allow kids to muddle through. We believe self-discovery is important, but more important, self-discovery needs to be shared. In this sharing process, it is reinforced. Unshared self-discovery is like edibles unconsumed, flowers unplanted, and jokes untold. As children develop problem-solving skills much beneficial learning can then be self-directed. That may very well be the pinnacle of education — that is, learning for the fun of it.

This book is about a system that is powerful and that will enable teachers to be effective; but the direction, either positive or negative, lies directly in the hands of the teacher. This system is not easy to implement; it is time-consuming and hard work. If used imprecisely, it can cause chaos in a matter of seconds. If excited kids learn better than docile, nonmotivated kids, then we'd better take the chance and excite them. We have structured classrooms where children are educationally dying. We have permissive schools where children are committing educational suicide. What we must develop is a classroom that will accommodate *individuals* and allow these individuals to function at their own rates and levels. More so, this model classroom must have a teacher that can reach all children and get all of them excited about learning. One way to do this is to provide the teacher with exciting, well planned things, ideas, and content to teach, accompanied with many methods and techniques of teaching. One of these methods is a token system.

Before proceeding to the specifics of what a token system is and how to develop and implement one, we would like to clarify several points:

1. It is discouraging when some teachers remark that they have tried a token system and it didn't work, when later we find their idea of a token system was handing out a token a week, or at best, a token a day for good behavior or for completing the arithmetic assignment. One of the first things that must be perfectly clear is that if you have not given out *at least* twenty-five tokens per child per day, you haven't used a token system. In order for the token system to work, you must communicate and communicate often. The same is true with praise. Some teachers say children don't respond to praise; but when you go to observe their classes, you find their rate of praises are quite low. When you bring this to their attention, they may respond with "I didn't have time," or "They didn't do anything worth praising." Well, in order to test whether tokens (or praises) work, they first have to be *given out, disseminated, dispensed.*

2. Sometimes token systems fail because the tokens can't be exchanged for anything that the child wants or that is worth getting. In this case, you will either have to find some desirable items or use a different system.

3. If a teacher feels uncomfortable setting goals for children and questions what behaviors are to be encouraged and what behaviors are not to be tolerated, then a token economy is *not* the technique for him to use. However, if a teacher thinks he knows what is good and right for kids to learn, feels very strongly that it is his job to facilitate their learning, has children that do not learn well through traditional instruction, then the token economy may be an effective teaching technique for him. The token economy is for the teacher who is directive-teacher oriented, who likes a certain amount of order in his room, who may even enjoy keeping logs, records, and charts on kids, and who enjoys seeing children earn special privileges and rewards. This teacher is the kind of person this system works best for.

Now let's proceed to chapter 2.

2

Using the Basic
Principles of
Behavior Modification

From the work of such forefathers of the behavior modification approach as Skinner, Homme, Ferster, and Lindsley, certain principles have evolved that aid in the precision with which behavior change can be made to occur. Many of these principles are just common sense. As you read them, if you stop for just a moment and reflect on a classroom situation, you will probably remember many instances in which they have been employed. We are all striving for precision in our teaching. The best way to achieve it while encountering the least amount of resistance is to make these principles an integral part of your response repertoire and use as many of them as possible as often as possible.

The major rules to follow that incorporate the basic principles of behavior modification include:

1. Keep the law of reinforcement firmly in mind throughout the day.

2. Reinforce a child when he exhibits desirable behavior and ignore him when he exhibits undesirable behavior.
3. Use positive reinforcement rather than punishment.
4. Reinforce desirable behavior immediately.
5. When first modifying a behavior apply a continuous schedule of reinforcement; later, after the behavior is acquired, gradually shift to an intermittent schedule.
6. Make high probability activities contingent on the performance of low probability activities.
7. Use the principle of pairing to expand your range of effective reinforcers.
8. Reward approximations toward the desired response.
9. When an action is desirable under specific circumstances, it should be reinforced only under those conditions.
10. If a behavior that has been reinforced to a high operant rate is no longer desirable, it can be extinguished by no longer reinforcing it.

1. *Keep the law of reinforcement firmly in mind throughout the day*

Deibert and Harmon (1970) have written a clear explanation of this basic law or principle of behavior.

> This basic law states that living organisms tend to repeat those behaviors that result in rewards (desirable outcomes) and tend to avoid those behaviors that fail to produce rewards. To state it another way, the "law of reinforcement" says: (1) Any behavior that is followed by a rewarding (desirable) outcome is likely to be repeated. The behavior is likely to *increase in frequency.* (2) Any behavior that is not followed by a reward will tend not to be repeated. The behavior is likely to *decrease in frequency....*
>
> To be consistent with the law of reinforcement we therefore have to assume that any behavior which is repeated again and again must be producing a reward (desired outcome). Otherwise, according to the law of reinforcement it would not occur. Only behaviors that produce rewards (desired outcomes) tend to be repeated. Therefore, if we observe a behavior occurring repeatedly, we have to assume that there is present in the situation some reward or desired outcome which supports it (p. 15).

According to the law of reinforcement, *behavior is learned as a result of environmental consequences.* Therefore, an effective way to change a person's behavior is to manipulate the environmental consequences which immediately follow his actions.

2. *Reinforce a child when he exhibits desirable behavior and ignore him when he exhibits undesirable behavior*

This statement seems, at first glance, self-evident. You certainly would not intentionally encourage a child to perform an undesirable behavior by the use of positive reinforcement.* It is not likely that you would want the rate of undesirable behavior to increase. However, the teacher without an adequate understanding of behavioral principles might unintentionally reinforce undesirable behavior. A common example is when a teacher argues with or pays attention to a child who exhibits undesirable behavior. The teacher, quite unaware of what is occurring, reinforces the child for his actions since he manages to gain the teacher's attention by displaying inappropriate behavior.

What should a teacher do when a child exhibits an undesirable behavior, such as playing with a toy during reading class? The immediate response might be to reprimand him. The teacher might consider this reprimand as punishment. Although it is aversive, the teacher is attending to the child and the child may interpret the reprimand as positive reinforcement, which is counter to the principle from the child's point of view. Remember that the rule states "reinforce a child when he exhibits desirable behavior and ignore him when he exhibits undesirable behavior." The natural question that follows would be "What should I do?" The answer is to ignore him, and reward the child when he exhibits desirable behavior.

To be even more effective, reinforce a behavior which is incompatible with the inappropriate behavior being exhibited while at the same time ignoring the inappropriate behavior. For example, a child who continuously gets out of his seat can be (1) reinforced for remaining in his seat and (2) ignored when he gets out of his seat. The child simply can not remain in his seat and out of his seat at the same time. We refer to this technique as the *double-barrelled approach.*

However, there are occasions when the undesirable behavior may be potentially harmful to the child himself or others and can not simply be ignored. For example, a child can not be allowed to throw rocks at his classmates. In a case such as this one, it may be best to place the child in an isolated area for a short period of time. This technique, which can be used to handle potentially dangerous and persistent types of undesirable behavior, is discussed more fully in chapter 3.

3. *Use positive reinforcement rather than punishment*

If a child is working to put a model ship together, he will work harder and put more effort into doing it correctly if he expects to receive a reward as a

---

*According to Buckley and Walker (1970), "a reinforcer is an event which *changes* behavior" (p.29). When the behavior is followed by a pleasurable event to the organism exhibiting the response, the consequence is termed *positive reinforcement*. According to Stephens (1970), "negative reinforcement...is a response to a behavior that is dissatisfying to the learner. Punishment and other forms of aversive techniques constitute negative reinforcers" (p.48).

In this book *reinforcement* will refer to positive reinforcement, unless otherwise explicitly stated.

result. He will also take pride in his work. However, the child who builds a ship only because he knows he will be punished if he does not may do a poor job, will not enjoy the work, may attach negative connotations to ship building, and will probably not like to build ships in the future. An analogy can be made from ship building to learning academic and social behaviors. For example, a child might attach a negative connotation to doing arithmetic if he is punished nearly every time he does one or two problems incorrectly. Using the positive method is not only more efficient and productive in terms of the outcome, but is also more conducive to future activities along the same lines.

Punishment can be used to extinguish a response. However, punishment has been found in some cases to have undesirable side effects. For example, if a child is punished, he may tend to avoid the punisher. Therefore, we strongly recommend the liberal use of positive reinforcement with little or no use of punishment.

4.   *Reinforce desirable behavior immediately*

Often six-week reports, academic honors at the end of the semester, pins for citizenship, and promotions at the end of the year are considered motivating devices for which children will strive every day of the school year. Is it reasonable to assume on the third day of school that a seven-year-old child will refrain from becoming angry at his peers who have been unkind to him so nine months later he can get his name on a good citizenship roll? This example may be a slight exaggeration, but many parents, administrators, and sometimes even teachers expect a piece of paper received several months later (an extremely long period of time for a child) to be strong enough motivation to cause a child to exhibit desirable behaviors during those several preceding months. Referring to our angry little friend, it is more probable that he would avoid an argument if he knew that by *not* arguing he would earn a cookie in half an hour. And wouldn't the incentive to avoid arguing be even stronger if he knew that he would get a token a minute or so later that he could exchange for a toy or something that he really wanted?

Children need immediate feedback concerning their actions. Many times, when even only a short time elapses before a child gets a reward, he may think that he received the reward for one behavior while in reality the teacher gave it to him for another. An example might be a teacher who gave a reward to a child for completing his work several minutes after he completed it. Since the child was cleaning his desk during the few minutes immediately after he completed his work and before he received the reward, he perceived that he received the reward for cleaning his desk. As a result, the number of times the child cleaned his desk increased while the teacher was actually interested in increasing the number of times the child completed his work. The child was confused, and the teacher lost faith in the system of rewards. This error in precision could have best been overcome by the teacher keeping firmly in mind the rule of reinforcing desirable behavior *immediately*. Don't allow time for intervening activities that may confuse the child. While immediacy is not always feasible, it should be adhered to as closely as possible.

5. *When first modifying a behavior apply a continuous schedule of reinforcement; later, after the behavior is acquired, gradually shift to an intermittent schedule*

Stephens (1970) has written a clear and easily understandable explanation of continuous and intermittent reinforcement.

> Continuous reinforcement is used when a reward is presented every time a desired response is given. After a response is established, the schedule should be changed so that reinforcement is not presented every time the desired response takes place. When this change is made, the schedule is then termed intermittent and it results in more stable behavior. Four types of intermittent schedules are described below:
>
> 1. Fixed-Interval Schedules: Once a response is established (which may require immediate reinforcement of every response), we can then reinforce it at certain clock intervals, every five minutes or every hour. Although the response rate becomes slower, the response is more stable and more immune to extinction, but another process sometimes intervenes. Immediately after reinforcement, the response rate may become lowered since no reinforcer is immediately forthcoming.
> 2. Variable-Interval Schedules: A low probability of response due to reinforcement on a fixed-interval schedule can be eliminated by using variable-interval reinforcement. Instead of reinforcing a response every ten minutes, we can vary it so that it is now one minute, now thirty minutes, etc., but averages every ten minutes. Using this type of schedule results in a response that is very difficult to extinguish.
> 3. Fixed-Ratio Schedules: Under fixed-ratio schedules reinforcement occurs every x number of responses. This is a quite inefficient schedule, for it results in long pauses between reinforcements, especially if the ratio of responses to reinforcement is high. To avoid long pauses after reinforcement, a schedule similar to a variable-interval one can be introduced.
> 4. Variable-Ratio Schedules: Variable-ratio schedules are highly efficient and hard to extinguish and produce high rates of responses. Under this schedule we may reinforce every second response at one time, and every 80th response at another time. The student has no way of anticipating when a response will be rewarded and therefore takes no chances.
>
> Note that intervals refer to *time* while ratios are used to designate *number*. Consequently, certain behaviors are more easily responded to

on a time basis while others lend themselves to use with frequency of occurrence (pp. 54-55).

Information as to when continuous and intermittent schedules of reinforcement should be applied is presented later in this book. Reasons for shifting from a continuous to an intermittent schedule are also stated.

6. *Make high probability activities contingent on the performance of low probability activities*

A low probability activity is one that a child generally would not want to do, while a high probability activity is one that a child would like to do. The high probability activity could be considered a reward while the low probability activity would be the desired behavior which the teacher wants the child to exhibit but which is of low preference for the child. The major point here is that the reward or high probability activity must be a strong enough motivator to get the child to exhibit the desired behavior. This principle is in operation when a child is told that he can play basketball for ten minutes *after* he completes ten arithmetic problems without an error. This principle is often referred to as the *Premack Principle*. See Premack (1959; 1965) and Homme (1969) for more information on this very important and useful principle.

7. *Use the principle of pairing to expand your range of effective reinforcers*

Some children will work long hours for such rewards as grades, stars, checkmarks, and tokens. However, in most cases, children desire these symbols or objects only after they have been associated with more basic or already learned reinforcers such as parent approval, certain privileges, candy, and toys. For example, a child who seems not to care what kind of grades he gets in school suddenly may become very concerned about his grades when told that he will receive five dollars for each *A* he earns. By pairing good grades with money, good grades became highly desirable and, therefore, reinforcing to the child. This principle will be applied when discussing how to shift from a token system to a primarily social reinforcement system later in this book.

8. *Reward approximations toward the desired response*

Generally, the appropriate response can be spotted and rewarded immediately, thus accelerating the rate of the response. There are cases, however, when a desired response is complex and involves several steps at once. A mistake at only one step may cause the end result to be incorrect. If a reward is provided at the completion of each individual step the child will be better able to understand and perform the desired behavior required. It will also facilitate more efficient learning of the entire response. An example of this principle is the command for a young child to go outside. Involved in this process are at least five steps:

1. Going to the door,
2. Opening the door,
3. Stepping outside,
4. Closing the door,
5. Walking down the steps.

The child could be rewarded at each of these five stages.

In short, the principle involves rewarding small approximations toward the desired response rather than withholding the reward until the child exhibits the complete response. This principle is sometimes referred to as *shaping*. It should be noted that individual differences among children in such characteristics as intelligence and age will determine the extent of breakdown necessary for the performance of complex tasks. Further discussion of this important concept is included in chapter 3.

9. *When an action is desirable under specific circumstances, it should be reinforced only under those conditions*

Certain behaviors may be appropriate or desirable in one situation while not in others. This concept is often difficult to convey to young children. An example of such a situation is when a child goes to Grandmother's house, he gets reinforced for talking by Grandmother's approval behaviors, as well as by candy and cookies. However, when he attends church services, his talkativeness is considered undesirable behavior. When he begins to talk, he is not positively reinforced and may possibly even be punished. The child is, of course, in a quandary. In such a case, rule 9 should be followed — only reward the behavior in the specific situation in which it is desirable. The child should be reinforced in one situation and never reinforced in the other for the specified behavior. After a few encounters with this type of reaction to the behavior, the child will begin to discriminate when talking is appropriate and when it is not.

Another, possibly even more efficient, means of handling such a case is to reinforce an opposing or competing response in the situation where the behavior is not appropriate. Going back to the child in church, if quiet behavior is reinforced, the talkative behavior will be reduced in order to get the reward for quiet behavior. The child can not talk and remain quiet at the same time. This rule suggests what needs to be done when in one situation the behavior is appropriate while in another situation the same behavior is inappropriate; the next rule suggests what needs to be done when at one time the behavior is appropriate, while at a later date the same behavior is inappropriate.

10.   *If a behavior that has been reinforced to a high operant rate is no longer desirable, it can be extinguished by no longer reinforcing it*

When a man is driving a car with a stick shift, he is reinforced when he changes gears by the car moving along properly and taking him where he wants to go. However, when he trades his stick shift in for an automatic car, he no longer needs to change gears the same way. If may even become an undesirable behavior since his transmission may be ruined. He will no longer be reinforced because the car will not move along properly and may not take him where he wants to go. Therefore, he stops trying to change gears — his "gear-shifting behavior" is extinguished. A behavior that was reinforced was extinguished when reinforcement was not provided.

In the classroom a child who is beginning to learn numbers may be reinforced in expressing the concepts by the use of his fingers. Later, however, as the child gains the ability to deal in abstractions, such use of the fingers might be considered undesirable. Reinforcement for using the fingers when counting can be withheld and finger counting will be extinguished.

Conclusion

Behavior modification principles have been applied throughout history. It is the precision with which an individual uses the principles that should be considered most critically. In other words, to modify behaviors in the most effective manner, precision is the clue. The principles discussed in this chapter can be noted throughout this book in explanations and suggestions although they are not explicitly stated.

Before proceeding to chapter 3, you should note that the material presented in this chapter is not meant to give you a comprehensive review of the principles of behavior modification, but to give you a brief introduction to some of the more basic principles. An understanding of behavior principles is essential. In fact, the successful establishment of a token system demands understanding and skill in applying the general principles of behavior modification as well as specific knowledge and skill regarding token system implementation. In other words, *the primary purpose of this book is to provide you with specific knowledge about what is involved in the establishment of a token system; however, a prerequisite to successfully applying the information presented is an adequate understanding of basic behavioral principles.* Therefore, we encourage you to gain additional knowledge regarding behavioral principles. A brief description of several books on behavior modification is presented in chapter 7.

References

Buckley, N. K. and H. M. Walker. *Modifying classroom behavior: A manual of procedure for classroom teachers.* Champaign, Ill.: Research Press, 1970.

Deibert, A. N. and A. J. Harmon. *New tools for changing behavior.* Champaign, Ill.: Research Press, 1970.

Homme, L., A. P. Csanyi, M. A. Gonzales, and J. R. Rechs. *How to use contingency contracting in the classroom.* Champaign, Ill.: Research Press, 1969.

Patterson, G. R. and M. E. Gullion. *Living with children: New methods for parents and teachers.* Champaign, Ill.: Research Press, 1968.

Premack, D. "Reinforcement theory." In D. Levine (ed.), *Nebraska symposium on motivation.* Lincoln, Nebr.: University of Nebraska Press, 1965.

———. "Toward empirical laws: Positive reinforcement. *Psychological Review* (1959), *66*, 219-33.

Stephens, T. M. *Directive teaching of children with learning and behavioral handicaps.* Columbus, Ohio: Charles E. Merrill Publishing Company, 1970.

Evaluation

You may choose to evaluate how well you comprehended the information presented in chapter 2 by responding to the following test items. Cover the answer column with a sheet of paper; then write your answers in the blank spaces provided. The correct answers may then be checked.

principles	1. Behavior change can be made to occur with more precision by using behavioral . . . .
increase in frequency	2. A behavior is likely to . . . . if it is followed by a reward.
decrease in frequency	3. A behavior is likely to . . . . if it is not followed by a reward.
environmental	4. Behavior is learned as a result of . . . . consequences.
manipulate consequences	5. An effective way to modify a child's behavior is to . . . . the environmental . . . . which immediately follow his actions.
reinforced	6. A child who displays desirable behavior should be . . . .
ignored	7. A child who is exhibiting undesirable behavior should be . . . .

incompatible

8. When trying to eliminate an undesirable behavior the teacher might decide to reinforce a behavior which is .... with the inappropriate behavior being displayed while at the same time ignoring the inappropriate behavior.

isolated

9. The child can be placed in a/an .... area for a short period of time when he exhibits an undesirable behavior that is potentially harmful to himself or others.

positive
punishment

10. It is better to use .... reinforcement while avoiding the use of ....

immediate
Reinforce

11. Children need.....................feedback concerning their actions. .... desirable behavior immediately.

continuous

12. A reward is given every time the desired response is displayed under a/an ....reinforcement schedule.

intermittent

13. Reinforcement is not presented every time the desired response is exhibited when a/an ....reinforcement schedule is in operation.

high probability

14. A child can be motivated, in many instances, to perform a low probability behavior by making the performance of a/an .... behavior contingent upon the performance of the low probability behavior.

pairing

15. Teachers can use the .... principle to increase the number of effective reinforcers available.

small
approximations

16. In some instances, reward .... toward the desired response instead of withholding the reward until the child exhibits the complete responses.

reinforced

17. If an action is appropriate under specific circumstances it should be .... only under those circumstances.

extinguished
reinforcing

18. A behavior that has received reinforcement and as a result has increased to a high operant rate can be .... by no longer ....it.

3

Answers to
Some Basic
Questions

A series of recent studies have demonstrated the effects of token systems*
on the classroom behavior of students. Bijou *et al.* (1966) increased
motivation, appropriate classroom conduct, and academic achievement of
retarded pupils through the introduction of a token economy. Hewett,
Taylor, and Artuso (1969) used a token system as part of their engineered
classroom design to enhance task attention and academic achievement of
emotionally disturbed children. Similarly, disruptive behavior of socially
maladjusted pupils has been reduced with token reinforcement
procedures (Kuypers, Becker, and O'Leary, 1968).

As it becomes apparent through applied research that token systems are
effective in the management of classroom behaviors, more teachers are

*The terms *token system, token economy,* and *token reinforcement* are used interchangeably
throughout. All three terms refer to a system which allows students, by demonstrating
specified types of behavior, to earn tokens that can be redeemed for selected items and activities attractive to the children.

17

beginning to establish such systems in their classrooms — unfortunately, in some cases, without the necessary practical knowledge or skill. The lack of knowledge is due, at least in part, to the paucity of articles and textbooks which discuss the practical considerations of implementing a token economy. Questions which typically go unanswered include:

1.   What should be used for tokens?
2.   When should tokens be dispensed?
3.   How many tokens need to be dispensed per child per day?
4.   Approximately how much does the establishment of a token economy cost?

The purpose of this chapter is to answer these and other questions which often arise when teachers attempt to initiate a token system. The answers are based on our experience in assisting teachers to establish token systems.

1.   *What, in general, is a token economy or system?*

A token economy in a classroom closely resembles the monetary reward system which operates in our free enterprise system. Students are rewarded (paid) for exhibiting behavior deemed appropriate by whomever is in authority. (The authority is the individual or group who regulates the reward and could be the teacher or the entire class operating under democratic principles.) Just as in the adult world we receive money or other tangible rewards for doing what our supervisor or society in general expects of us, children can earn tokens for doing what the teacher or their peers expect of them. And just as money can be exchanged for goods, clothes, shelter, food, cars, and entertainment, tokens can be redeemed for items attractive to children.

2.   *What is the major difference between token and social reinforcement?*

Under a token system, children who behave appropriately or achieve academically receive tokens, chips, checkmarks, etc., which are exchangable (redeemable) for something tangible such as candy, toys, or pleasing activities. Social reinforcement, on the other hand, rewards children with kisses, attention, praise, and other displays of love and approval for exhibiting appropriate behavior. Unfortunately the dispensation of social reinforcers alone will not always produce change in children's behavior. If a child, because of a poor relationship with his teacher, does not care what the teacher says or does, attention and praise are not likely to be very effective in motivating the child to achieve or behave. Therefore, it may be advisable in such cases to initiate a token system in the early stages of attempting to change a child's behavior. A child may be weaned from a token system to a social reinforcement system, if so desired, by combining social reinforcers with token reinforcers and very gradually employing more and more social reinforcers while supplying fewer tangible reinforcers.

3. What type of reinforcement schedule works best?

The terms *continuous* and *intermittent* reinforcement are common in the literature on behavior modification. However, information as to when these reinforcement schedules should be employed in a token economy is often hard to find.

A continuous schedule is in operation when a child is reinforced every time he exhibits the specified behavior. Although this schedule of reinforcement is applied frequently in laboratory experiments, from a practical standpoint it is impossible to reinforce on a continuous schedule in the classroom. One teacher can not observe and reinforce all the specified appropriate behaviors of all the children in his class unless only one or two children are enrolled. In the typical classroom, it is entirely likely that the specified behaviors could be exhibited and go unnoticed and thus not receive reinforcement. Nevertheless, during the early weeks of a token program you should try to *adhere as closely as possible to a continuous schedule.* The idea is to get the children succeeding and therefore hooked on the reinforcers.

Later you will want to gradually shift to an intermittent schedule, in which reinforcement is not given after every response to maintain the behaviors acquired. Descriptions of four different intermittent reinforcement schedules were included in chapter 2. There are two primary reasons for transferring to an intermittent schedule.

1. Behavior maintained by an intermittent schedule has a greater resistance to extinction.
2. An intermittent schedule is easier for the teacher to administer since he does not have to attempt to reinforce each child every time he exhibits the appropriate behavior.

4. What is the reinforcer in a token economy?

A reinforcer is the payoff that changes the child's behavior. In some instances, the tokens themselves will change children's behavior without being exchangeable for more pleasing items, just as some children will work for gold stars, grades, or stamps. However, tokens usually become reinforcing only when they are paired and therefore associated with food, candy, toys, and other appealing items. When selecting items to serve as basic reinforcers it is imperative to ascertain what is desirable and attractive to each child. What appeals to one child may not appeal to another, and if nothing you have available for basic reinforcement is attractive to a child, a token economy is not likely to change his behavior.

One way of determining what a child likes is to ask him. Another way is to record what each child buys with his tokens. The items the child buys the most often are probably what he likes the best. A third way would be to construct a reinforcement menu and have the children select the items they would like to earn.

5. *What kinds of behavior should be of concern to the teacher?*

Madsen and Madsen (1970) defined behavior as anything a person does, says, or thinks that can be directly or indirectly observed. In addition, they stated, "A well behaved child is a child that behaves in ways the teacher thinks are appropriate to the situation" (p. 17). Assuming this definition is correct, the behaviors that should be reinforced are those which the teacher feels are appropriate, if he desires to have well behaved students. These behaviors might include sitting quietly at desk, raising hand before speaking out, or completing an assignment.

Kuypers, Becker, and O'Leary (1968) wrote that one way to make a token system fail is to dispense tokens for meeting an absolute standard rather than for improvement. Deibert and Harmon (1970) stated:

> Instead of expecting a child to perform a complex behavioral response on his first few attempts a *shaping* approach should be used. The task should be analyzed and an attempt made to determine the various steps or parts of which it consists. We then arrange these parts of the response in a series. We place them in a natural order from the most basic or elementary part of the behavior proceeding through in step-wise fashion to the complete response. Each part requires a little more of the child than the one preceding. The child performs the first part of the response. After he is performing this part easily, we require the next step. Again, he is given time to learn this part of it well. Additional steps are required until he has been gradually shaped into performing the complex behavior or task. Of course, it is understood that each step or unit is followed by a *reward* (p. 34).

6. *What is the best way to observe behavior?*

In order to know if the frequency of a behavior has increased or decreased, you must know how often it has occurred in the past as well as how often it is presently occurring. Behavior is primarily measured in terms of frequency of occurrence; that is, when a teacher evaluates a particular behavior, he counts the number of times the behavior appears. The counting usually takes place within a specified time interval. To measure academic behaviors, formal and informal tests are often employed. For example, children are given an arithmetic test of ten problems to do in twenty minutes, and the number of problems they get right or wrong is counted. Although social behavior is a little more difficult to observe, it can and must be done if you are to know whether a particular behavior is decreasing, increasing, or remaining stable.

If you would like to discourage a group of children from leaving their seats, the first step would be to count the exact number of times the children actually get out of their seats in a designated time interval. The counting may be done during any seat work activity. It is advisable to count and record the number of out-of-seat behaviors two or three days before attempting to change the behavior. Hitting, shoving, pushing, speaking out of turn, sharpening pencils, crying, or almost any other observable behavior can be recorded in the same manner. The primary prerequisite for recording such behaviors is that they be precisely defined in observable terms in order that you know exactly what you are counting. It may be advisable to count the behaviors when the children are engaged in the same type of activity each day. They might display differing amounts of a specified behavior during reading than during physical education because of the differing nature of the classes.

Remember to concentrate on only one or two behaviors at a time unless you have a great deal of assistance and/or experience. A priority list can be made and the most unsavory types of actions can be dealt with first. The frequency of a behavior should be measured before and after you attempt to change the behavior; otherwise, you will have no way to determine whether the attempt was successful. An illustration of what can be obtained by counting the frequency of a behavior during a specified time interval is the case of Robert, a ten-year-old boy who continuously gets out of his seat. In order to change this out-of-seat behavior his teacher decides to dispense tokens to him for exhibiting an incompatible behavior, i.e., remaining in his seat. After counting and recording out-of-seat behavior during a ten-minute interval the first day (baseline), he begins dispensing tokens for *in-seat behavior*. He continues to record the frequency of Robert's out-of-seat behavior each day during a ten minute interval for the next four days.

He then constructs a graph, Figure 1, in order to have a clear picture of what changes in behavior were acquired. It can be seen in Figure 1 that out-of-seat behavior for Robert occurred twenty times the first day, five times the second, five times the third, three times the fourth, and one time the fifth day. We would conclude that Robert's out-of-seat behavior decreased considerably during the five days under consideration.

In this illustration, we purposely decided that the teacher would observe for a ten-minute time period each day. But what if we had decided to have him observe various lengths of time each day? (A teacher might have

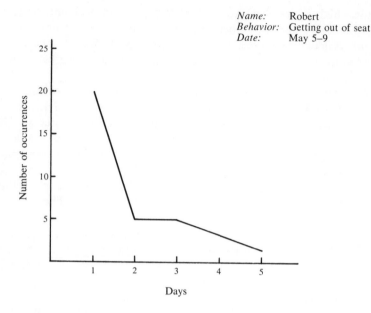

FIGURE 1.   *Out-of-seat behavior during a ten minute interval.*

various amounts of free time over a designated number of days.) It would then be useful to compute the rate at which the behavior occurs. The number of times a behavior is occurring per minute can be easily ascertained by using the formula:

$$\text{rate per minute} = \frac{\text{number of occurrences}}{\text{number of minutes observed}}$$

If Susan is observed hitting Billy thirty times during a fifteen-minute time period, we could compute by this formula that she hits him two times per minute (2 = 30/15). See Buckley and Walker (1970) for additional information regarding the measurement of behavior.

7.   When should tokens be dispensed?

Tokens should be given immediately following the designated desired behavior. *A common mistake is to wait too long.*

You will soon discover that when attempting to bring a child behaving inappropriately under control, it is sometimes very effective to reinforce someone near him who is behaving. This action lets him know in a subtle way that he is missing tokens by continuing to act inappropriately. However, this practice can be dangerous and requires extreme care. If the other children catch on, they might enter into an agreement whereby one child will consent to misbehave so that the children sitting around him will receive tokens. His price, of course, is a certain number of tokens from each child.

8.   What should be done about undesirable behavior?

The two most common ways to handle undesirable behavior are to ignore it and to punish it. When ignoring, do not argue or debate with the child; that is, pay no attention to him while he is exhibiting the undesirable behavior. Never under any circumstances give a token to a child who displays undesirable behavior. However, remember to reinforce *appropriate behaviors* immediately when again exhibited by the child in question.

A method of punishment which has been employed as an effective way to weaken undesirable behavior is *time-out*. When a child acts inappropriately he is told that he will have to spend a certain amount of time, usually five or six minutes, in isolation. It is important to tell the child the specific amount of time and that if he misbehaves during the isolation period he will have to remain an extra period of time. The area designated as the time-out area should not be reinforcing and should be totally secluded. A completely bare room with only a light and a chair would serve best. Once you have put a child into the isolation area be sure to continue to put him there every time he demonstrates the same behavior. Consistency is essential. The reader is referred to Patterson and Gullion (1968) for an additional discussion concerning the use of time-out sessions.

Another means of punishment is to take tokens away for misbehavior. We recommend that this be done as infrequently as possible. It is much better to keep children working for positive reinforcement rather than to avoid a negative consequence.

Among the many possible inappropriate behaviors, two inevitably occur when a token economy is implemented. Sooner or later a child will *ask for a token*. This behavior is inappropriate and should be treated as such. Another undesirable behavior that eventually occurs is that a child will test the system by saying something like "I don't like those old tokens you are giving out and I don't want any more of them." You should respond to these behaviors just as you would to any other undesirable or inappropriate behavior — by ignoring them completely. Remember, it is imperative that you don't argue with, debate, or pay attention to the child exhibiting such behaviors in any way.

9.   Is there any particular way tokens should be dispensed?

There are certain procedures that should be followed. Go to the child and place the token in his hand or on his desk. Do not have the child come to you. At the beginning of each new activity dispense a large number of tokens and gradually decrease the number being given after the children come under control. Smile and have physical contact with the child. One way to accomplish this is to place your hand on his shoulder and smile when you give him tokens. In the initial stages, say aloud the reasons for the dispensation of tokens so that every child in the room will be fully aware of the reasons. Make your sentences clear, concise and to the point: "I like the way you are sitting quietly." Do not complicate them with unnecessary verbiage, such as "Here is a token because I like the way you are sitting quietly." Occasionally socially reinforce a child without dispensing a token. These last three procedures will make it easier to shift to a social reinforcement system if you want to.

10. *Should the children be allowed to play with the tokens they have earned?*

There is no real harm in allowing children to play with the tokens they have acquired during the first day or two of a token program, since it will give them an opportunity to see and touch what they have earned. This activity seems to make the tokens more valuable to them. However, it can become a problem if the children continue to play with their tokens beyond the initial stage. They might, for instance, tend to manipulate their tokens when they should be attending to a specific task. Rewarding those children who have their tokens off the top of their desk and out of the way will normally stop this type of activity.

11. *What should be used for tokens?*

Heavy or awkward objects should be avoided. While it makes little difference what is used for tokens, it is important that they be attractive, light-weight, durable, and easy to handle and dispense. Examples would be poker chips, chips from Peabody Language Development Kits, or buttons. Because a large number of tokens are dispensed to each child, ease of handling is especially important.

12. *Will children steal tokens from each other?*

Most children will not steal. If it is suspected that a child is stealing, tokens of a unique color can be given to him. When the children exchange their tokens for basic reinforcers, this child should of course be allowed to turn in only tokens of the same color dispensed to him. His stealing will probably diminish when he finds there is nothing to be gained. One alternative to using different colored tokens would be to let the child steal. Most children will learn very quickly under these circumstances to make provisions to protect their own tokens.

13. *Should tokens be dispensed on a group or individual basis?*

When a group of children have the ability to perform equally well in relation to a particular task, it would be appropriate to reinforce them as a group. However, children often differ in their abilities, and the dispensation of tokens should be individualized just as instruction should. Regardless of the level on which an individual child happens to be performing, he should be given a token when he makes an improvement.

A note of caution should be added here. If you reinforce children on a group basis, it is essential to be absolutely sure that every child in the group has exhibited the behavior that is being reinforced. Since it is almost impossible to observe each child in a group of children simultaneously, we strongly recommend that you refrain, in most cases, from dispensing tokens on a group basis.

14. *What is the best way to keep an accurate account of the number of tokens given each child?*

Efficient record-keeping procedures can save time and trouble. There is probably no one best way to do this, but we have found several methods which appear to be fairly efficient. One is to have your aide (if you have one) count the number of tokens earned by each child at the end of each day and enter the number on a recording sheet. If you do not have an aide

Name	Mon.	Tues.	Wed.	Thurs.	Fri.	Total
1.						
2.						
3.						
4.						
5.						
6.						
7.						
8.						
9.						
10.						
11.						
12.						
13.						
14.						
15.						
16.						
17.						
18.						

FIGURE 2.   Recording sheet for number of tokens earned.

you will have to take five or ten minutes at the end of each day to do this task. Most students can be taught to perform this task. Counting and recording the number of tokens earned by each child can be a meaningful and practical learning experience for some children. Figure 2 illustrates how a recording sheet may be organized.

15.   *How many tokens are normally dispensed in a regular school day?*

It is better to dispense too many tokens than too few, especially at first. The objective is to get the students behaving and achieving as soon as possible. Most people, for some reason, tend to be stingy with the tokens — they hoard them. It is imperative then, to remember to give out large numbers of tokens. Twenty-five to seventy-five tokens for each child on the first day is not excessive. The person giving out the tokens must search out appropriate behavior. Catch children being good and reward them immediately. To insure that you do not end up hoarding all the tokens, you must learn to be forgiving and not to hold grudges. If a child displays an undesirable behavior or a series of inappropriate behaviors at ten o'clock one morning you cannot ignore him for the remainder of the day. He should be watched carefully and rewarded immediately when he exhibits appropriate behavior. In this way he will begin to work for tokens instead of spending the entire day challenging the system by displaying undesirable behavior.

16.   *How can I dispense tokens and teach at the same time?*

It would be foolish to pretend that this is not a difficult task. Nevertheless, we have learned that it can be done successfully. The use of a timer can help make the job possible. Almost any easy-to-handle mechanical device that can be set to ring at random intervals (averaging five to seven minutes) can be used as a timer. When the timer rings you can stop whatever you are doing and dispense tokens to those children who have exhibited appropriate behavior *during* the preceeding time interval.

Another way, easier and more efficient, is to have your aide, if you have one, dispense the tokens. He should be specifically instructed when, and for what, to dispense tokens.

Finally, your job will be much simpler if you arrange your classroom so that you can see most of the children most of the time. Classroom management will be discussed in more detail in chapter 4.

If it is not feasible for you to dispense a minimum of twenty-five tokens per child per day, then we would suggest that you not even attempt to establish such a system in your classroom. An alternative to a token system could be a contingency contract system, such as the one which is explained by Homme in *How to Use Contingency Contracting in the Classroom.* (1969).

17. *What is a store and with what should it be stocked?*

A store is exactly what its name implies. It could resemble on a small scale any real store, stocked with a wide variety of items. A store constructed as part of a token economy often stocks such items as perfume, candy, lotions, jewelry, lipstick, combs, crayons, pencils, paper, magnets, and footballs. Almost anything that could be attractive to children might be included. The most important aspect to consider when choosing the stock is whether the items will appeal to the children for whom they are being selected. Of course, safety, practicality, and price of the merchandise must also be taken into account.

It is best to stock the store with many edible items in the initial stages. A small chocolate candy bar, for instance, can be consumed on the spot, quickly providing immediate reinforcement. The child, as a result, learns rapidly that the basic reinforcers are really worth achieving. A toy, which can not be played with until after school, does not provide the immediate reinforcement that consumable items do.

18. *What is all this going to cost in cold cash?*

Surprisingly, the establishment of a token economy is not as expensive as most people think. The actual expense will depend to some extent on the characteristics and backgrounds of the children being served — especially their age and socioeconomic level. We have found that a store can, in most cases, be adequately stocked for $.15 to $.20 per child per week. For a group of fifteen to twenty children a classroom can operate on a token economy for as little as $3.00 initial store outlay plus $2.25 per week operational cost. A teacher with good community relations can usually defray a large portion of the cost through actively seeking donations from various businesses, organizations, and clubs. Basically, the actual cost of a token system is directly related to the number of tokens charged per item, which is determined by the amount of money you have to spend.

19. *How many tokens should be charged for various items?*

The number of tokens charged for an item should be directly related to the cost of the item. Adequately stocked stores have a wide variety of merchandise worth from a penny to a dollar or more. A quick and easy method to determine token-cost per item is to add at least one zero to the actual cost of an item. Under this system, a penny piece of candy would be worth ten tokens and a five-cent piece, fifty tokens; while a fifty-cent bottle of hand lotion would be worth five hundred. These prices are meant only as examples. The number of tokens charged for each item should fit your own budget and situation. A precise method for determining token-cost per item would be to use this formula:

$$
\begin{array}{c}
\text{number of} \\
\text{children} \\
\text{in class}
\end{array}
\times
\begin{array}{c}
\text{estimated tokens} \\
\text{dispensed per} \\
\text{child per day}
\end{array}
\times
\begin{array}{c}
\text{school days} \\
\text{per week}
\end{array}
=
\begin{array}{c}
\text{number of tokens} \\
\text{to charge per} \\
\text{penny}
\end{array}
$$

amount of money the teacher has
to spend per week (in cents)

A teacher knows the number of children in his class, the estimated number of tokens he wants to give out per child per day, the number of school days per week, and the amount of money he has to spend per week. It is therefore a simple arithmetic calculation to figure the token-cost per penny. For instance, let's say a teacher has fifteen children, plans to dispense approximately fifty tokens per child per day, has a five-day school week, and has $2.00 to spend. He can figure the token-cost per penny in the following manner:

$$\frac{15 \times 50 \times 5}{200} = \text{no. of tokens to charge per penny}$$

$$\frac{3750}{200} = \text{no. of tokens to charge per penny}$$

$$18.75 = \text{no. of tokens to charge per penny}$$

In this example the teacher would charge nineteen or twenty tokens per penny, i.e., a penny piece of candy would cost twenty tokens, a five-cent candy bar would cost one hundred tokens, and a fifty-cent jack-ball set would cost one thousand tokens.

Regardless of the method used for figuring token-cost per item, a record should be kept of what each child buys, in order to determine what is selling and what is not. In this way you will not buy a lot of merchandise that does not appeal to children. However, no matter how careful you are, you will sooner or later buy some things that the children do not want to purchase at the price you are charging. If it is apparent that a few items are not selling very well over a rather long period of time, a sale can be held and these particular items sold for two-thirds or one-half the tokens normally charged.

In addition to selling merchandise there are many items that can be rented, such as record players, tape recorders, radios, and the various games available in most classrooms. Johnny might be allowed to pay thirty tokens to rent the record player for fifteen minutes. Time to engage in a highly desired activity such as playing basketball outside for ten or fifteen minutes can also be sold.

We would like to make it perfectly clear that it *is* possible to operate a token economy at almost no cost when items and privileges are used that are of no cost to the teacher or school district. Typical types of free items and privileges that have been successfully used by teachers are helping the teacher in various ways, distributing the tokens or keeping store, extended recess, running and yelling, field trips, eating lunch in the classroom, tutoring younger children, and feeding the class pets. Many teachers implement token systems with no money by using such rewards.

20. How often should redemption of tokens occur?

Redemption of tokens should probably take place once or twice each day during the first three or four days of a token economy. In this way the children are made aware of the real value of tokens shortly after receiving them. However, a goal of having store only once a week should be slowly worked toward. The children can afford to redeem their tokens more frequently during the first week, because a large number of tokens (as many as twenty-five to seventy-five per day) are dispensed to each child during the earlier stages of a token economy. This number is gradually reduced until it stabilizes at approximately fifteen to thirty tokens per child per day. (The numbers quoted are what we have found to be about average; the actual number will vary from one program to another and from one child to another.)

Two events happen frequently enough in relation to redemption of tokens to deserve special attention. First, nearly every child will sooner or later ask to go to the store at a time other than that scheduled. If he is allowed to go, other children will be asking to go soon afterwards. Remember that when you answer such a question, especially in the affirmative, its frequency will tend to increase. Therefore, if you do not want to be replying to this question frequently each day, simply say no. Second, children will ask if they can save their tokens. This certainly does no harm, and may result in some interesting learning. In fact, we imagine that a lot of children can learn to put "something away for a rainy day" when placed in a position of being responsible for the tokens they spend and save.

21. Why bother with the establishment of a token economy?

When inappropriate behaviors have been reinforced over a long period of time, a concrete, clear, and precise system of communication is needed when attempting to make a radical change. In addition, when a student, for whatever reasons, does not trust authority figures, he sometimes will tend not to hear what they say — including what is positive. Tokens are a highly visible means of communicating to the child that appropriate behaviors will be rewarded.

Some students exhibit what seems to be, at first glance, such a low frequency of appropriate behaviors that we have a hard time using lots of praise and attention even when trying to do so. When employing a token economy, if you end the day with one child having only two or three tokens, you know that you have to watch the child more closely the next day and catch him exhibiting appropriate behavior. If each child does not have twenty-five to seventy-five tokens, you have done a poor job of seeking out appropriate behavior. Finally, the implementation of a token economy helps train you, the teacher, in the precise use of behavior modification principles. It requires that you focus attention on appropriate behaviors while ignoring undesirable behaviors.

According to Ayllon and Azrin (1968):

> Tokens have several valuable features as conditioned reinforcers: (1) The number of tokens can bear a simple quantitative relation to the amount of reinforcement; (2) the tokens are portable and can be in the subject's possession even when he is in a situation far removed from that in which the tokens were earned; (3) no maximum exists in the number of tokens a subject may possess, whereas dimensions such as intensity, as with volume of music, have practical maximum reinforcing value; (4) tokens can be used directly to operate devices for the automatic delivery of reinforcers; (5) tokens are durable and can be continuously present during the delay, in contrast, say, with a brief flash of light or sound; (6) the physical characteristics of the tokens can be easily standardized; (7) the tokens can be made fairly indestructible so they will not deteriorate during the delay; (8) the tokens can be made unique and nonduplicable so that the experimenter can be assured that they are received only in the authorized manner. In addition, the token has the usual advantages of other conditioned reinforcers: (1) It bridges the delay between the desired response and the delivery of reinforcement, thereby maintaining the response in strength; (2) it allows the response to be reinforced any time, whereas primary reinforcement is typically restricted as to time and place; (3) it allows sequences of responses to be reinforced without interruption due to delivery of the reinforcer (p. 77).

22.   *Should social reinforcers be used in conjunction with tokens?*

Yes, verbal praise and attention should be combined with tokens. After the children learn appropriate behaviors via a token system, most teachers attempt to wean them away from a token system and toward a social reinforcement system. If praise, attention, and other displays of approval have been combined with the dispensation of tokens, the move from a token to a social reinforcement system will be easier.

Conclusion

The questions and answers presented are not meant to be comprehensive. However, it is hoped that they will serve to provide a few clues as to what is involved from a practical standpoint in the successful implementation of a token system. In addition, it would be good to keep the following points in mind.

The establishment of a token economy is not a substitute for good teaching, nor is it a panacea for all of education's problems. It is a tool that can help shape behavior. When utilizing a planned behavior modification approach, interesting, exciting, and meaningful lessons should be geared to the ability level of each child. Children could be required to learn dull and meaningless materials under a token system; however, this would be a misuse of the system.

Token systems can be implemented for one child, a specific group of children, or an entire class. Of course, the larger the number of children involved, the greater the amount of assistance you will need in dispensing tokens, evaluating behavior, and keeping records.

Although the operation of a token economy is considered impersonal and cold by some, the gains made as a result of such a system can allow you to be very human and warm, since the system often reduces the disciplinary problems that sometimes lead to strained relationships between teacher and student.

Token reinforcement is a powerful tool — one that can create as well as solve problems. Therefore, it is imperative that both you and the students know exactly what behavior you are reinforcing. The following incident occurred the first time one of the authors participated in a token system. After dispensing tokens for approximately fifteen or twenty minutes, he noticed that nearly all of the children were raising their hands, getting out of their seats, and tiptoeing back and forth to the pencil sharpener. He had given a token to a child for raising his hand and asking to go to the pencil sharpener. After the child quietly went to the pencil sharpener and back to his seat he was given another token. Obviously, the other children caught on quickly. In a few minutes, to the teacher's surprise, he observed the entire class tiptoeing back and forth to the pencil sharpener. The successful establishment of a token economy calls for industry, patience, knowledge, and skill. Nevertheless, it has been our experience that when used with some degree of consistency the results are most gratifying.

References

Ayllon, T. and N. Azrin. *The token economy.* New York: Appleton-Century-Crofts, 1968.

Bijou, S. W., J. S. Birnbrauer, J. D. Kidder, and C. E. Tague. "Programmed instruction as an approach to teaching of reading, writing and arithmetic to retarded children." *Psychological Record* (1966), *16,* 505-22.

Buckley, N. K. and H. W. Walker. *Modifying classroom behavior: A manual of procedure for classroom teachers.* Champaign, Ill.: Research Press, 1970.

Deibert, A. N. and A. J. Harmon. *New tools for changing behavior.* Champaign, Ill.: Research Press, 1970.

Hewett, F., F. Taylor, and A. Artuso. "The Santa Monica project: Evaluation of an engineered classroom dealing with emotionally disturbed children." *Exceptional Children* (1969), *35*, 101-9.

Homme, L. *How to use contingency contracting in the classroom.* Champaign, Ill.: Research Press, 1969.

Keller, F. S. *Learning: Reinforcement theory.* New York: Random House, Inc., 1969.

Kuypers, D. S., W. C. Becker, and K. D. O'Leary. "How to make a token system fail." *Exceptional Children* (1968), *35*, 101-9.

Madsen, D. H. and C. K. Madsen. *Teaching/discipline: Behavioral principles toward a positive approach.* Boston: Allyn and Bacon, Inc., 1970.

Patterson, G. R. and E. M. Gullion. *Living with children: New methods for parents and teachers.* Champaign, Ill.: Research Press, 1968.

Evaluation

You may want to take a few moments and see if you can now answer the questions that were asked in chapter 3. Write the answers on a separate piece of paper. After you respond, compare your answer with the answer given by the authors.

1. What, in general, is a token economy or system?
2. What is the major difference between token and social reinforcement?
3. What type of reinforcement schedule works best?
4. What is the reinforcer in a token economy
5. What kinds or types of behavior should be of concern to the teacher?
6. What is one way to observe behavior?
7. When should tokens be dispensed?
8. What should be done about undesirable behavior?
9. Is there any particular way tokens should be dispensed?
10. Should the children be allowed to play with the tokens they have earned?
11. What should be used for tokens?
12. Will children steal tokens from each other?
13. Should tokens be dispensed on a group or individual basis?
14. What is one way to keep an accurate account of the number of tokens given each child?

15. How many tokens are normally dispensed in a regular school day?
16. How can I dispense tokens and teach at the same time?
17. What is a store and with what should it be stocked?
18. What is all this going to cost in cold cash?
19. How many tokens should be charged for various items?
20. How often should redemption of tokens occur?
21. Why bother with the establishment of a token economy?
22. Should social reinforcers be used in conjunction with tokens?

4

Step-by-Step
Procedure

Often when a teacher is interested in implementing a token system, he must rely on haphazard guessing as to how he should set up his program. He is aware that the children must be reinforced and that the reinforcement must be meaningful, but what he does first or second in the sequence of program development is left to sheer intuition. It is, therefore, our objective in this chapter to present a step-by-step analysis of how a token system can be implemented. This is only one method; as in most programs, there are several ways to proceed. However, this method has worked, and we have found it effective and efficient.

This chapter is divided into two sections. Nine steps that should be taken before establishing a token economy are presented first. The second section consists of day-by-day procedures that can be followed when actually implementing a token economy.

Steps Before
Implementation

1. *Become familiar with behavior modification generally and token systems specifically*

Before an individual sets out to do any job, including implementing a token system, it is helpful for him to learn how it has been done by an experienced person. The teacher must be familiar with what he is trying to accomplish and can learn from fellow professionals experienced in token economies. We assume that you are reading this book to learn something about a token system; remember, it should be read in its entirety before implementing a token program. In addition to this material, you should read about behavior modification programs that others have established and problems they have encountered. Abstracts and descriptions of articles and books containing such information are provided in chapter 7. Reading chapter 7 can aid you in choosing literature applicable to your particular situation. Read the original sources that interest you the most for a more in-depth understanding.

Films concerning behavior modification and its use can usually be obtained from school systems, colleges, universities, or libraries. These films can be reviewed, possibly even several times, to see the methods and precision used by experienced and skilled teachers. A list of films is also included in chapter 7 for your convenience.

Another source of information might be classes in your school system or in surrounding cities and counties in which token programs have already been established. Talk to the teacher, watch the system in operation, and if the opportunity presents itself, get involved by such means as distributing tokens to get experience and first-hand information. Remember, read and learn as much as possible before attempting to establish a program yourself.

2. *Arrange the setting for effective and efficient implementation*

Arrangement of the setting is a common occurrence in everyday life. People are constantly arranging settings — whether it be a living room, office, cafeteria, or classroom — to provide a conducive atmosphere for their activity. An example might be a living room. You certainly would not put a television in a room with the screen facing the wall or a chair in front of the television so that it would block the view of the screen from other sitting positions. Since a living room is often used as a comfortable place to carry on conversations and watch television, most people arrange it so that it will be conducive to the efficient and effective means of achieving its purposes.

Your classroom must be arranged in such a way as to be conducive to the implementation of a token system. The best way to determine the correct arrangement is to consider the activities that need to be carried on and set up the room accordingly. Since the teacher must be aware of each child's actions at every moment, arrange your desk so that you can see each child from every point in the room. Small meeting areas, as for reading groups, should be set up so that you can easily see the remaining children in their seats while conducting such meetings. This warning may seem a bit trite, but many teachers work in small groups with their backs to the remainder of the class to help eliminate distracting sounds or movements. If tokens are going to be dispensed for appropriate behavior then the teacher must place himself in a position to observe as much behavior as possible.

The ability to see the children should also be considered when writing on the board. Try to put all needed information on the board before the school day begins. If this is not possible, a useful aid would be an overhead projector. Overlays of assignments could be made ahead of time. If for an explanation writing needs to be done, it is not difficult to stand at the side and write on the overlay while the children are still in visual range. If such equipment is not available, a large mirror can be hung above the blackboard to help you see the children.

Another aspect necessary for the proper implementation of a token system is immediate reinforcement of appropriate behaviors, which requires that the aisles and desks be arranged so that any point in the room is quickly and easily accessible. The student should not be required to wait for his reinforcement.

These are just a few of the considerations that must be taken into account. As you read the principles and techniques presented throughout this book, other modifications of the classroom setting will become apparent and you, as the teacher in the classroom, will be best able to apply the needed changes.

3. *Obtain appropriate tokens*

Tokens are those objects that are used as immediate reinforcers for appropriate behavior exhibited. They are usually of no real value in themselves; however, they take on value when they are exchangeable for desirable objects. They might be considered the same as money for the working man or woman. Hence, tokens can be considered the form of currency employed in a token economy.

Like money, tokens should not be easy to duplicate. If they can be easily duplicated, just as with money, forgeries will begin to appear in the classroom and your system will break down. Children will no longer need to display the appropriate behaviors to get their currency. Therefore, this characteristic must be seriously considered.

One good type of tokens, the one we generally employed, is chips from Peabody Language Development Kits. They are easy for the teacher to obtain while not being directly accessible to the children. Generally, they can be secured by most teachers from Peabody Kits within their school, surrounding schools, or directly from the American Guidance Service.*

The number of tokens needed will range anywhere from 1000 to 4000, depending on the size of the class. If you estimate 100 for each child, you can be reasonably assured that you have an adequate number, assuming that you have the children turn in their tokens at the end of each day, with credit being given for tokens earned.

An alternative to tokens is a card taped to each child's desk or a notebook for each child. On the card or notebook you can make a tally mark each time the child displays an appropriate behavior, thus eliminating the need to carry a large number of tokens. This set-up should have the same applicable characteristics of the tokens. One advantage of tokens, however, is that the child has tangible, manipulatable objects to show for his appropriate behaviors. For some children, this concreteness appears to be important. Remember, as the teacher you are in the best position to make the decision as to the type of tokens to be used.

4. *Establish your store*

The store incorporates all that is involved in the process of token exchange. The teacher must consider what items will be available, price of the items, store hours, where the transactions will take place, and bookkeeping procedures. The quality of the store you set up will determine to a large degree the strength of the system. The more desirable the items included in the store, the harder the children will work to obtain them. Since the items presented for sale are usually the motivation for the children, the selection of these items is extremely important. What is highly reinforcing for one child may be of little value to another. Careful observation of each child should, therefore, precede the purchase of any items.

Other considerations include the amount of money that can be spent and the availability of inexpensive items. We suggest that the teacher explore every possibility for obtaining free items and financial assistance. Also, merchandise can consist of renting items already available in your classroom, such as blackboard space, record players, or tape recorders, for short periods of time during the day. These rentals will expand the selection at no cost to the system. In the beginning, many inexpensive

---

*American Guidance Service, Inc., Dept. E-9, Publisher's Building, Circle Pines, Minn. 55014.

items should be available in the store so the children will not have to wait to start winning in the system. After the children have begun to reap the benefits of the program, higher priced items can be made available and the children can begin to save their tokens to purchase these items.

The store can be presented in several ways. The teacher may conduct the store from his desk or from a table in another area of the room. A decorated box can be used as a distribution center or items may simply be displayed on any flat surface. Children enjoy an attractive arrangement and colorful price list; however, any arrangement that has the qualities of efficiency and effectiveness can be employed. Initially, the store should be held quite often, while in the latter stages more time can elapse between open times. This scheduling is another means of aiding the children to profit in the beginning.

Bookkeeping procedures, although they appear to be secondary, are important. After the first few days, children tend to begin saving and, in some cases, hoarding their tokens. Since the children can not keep all of the tokens they collect (for example, over a week's time), a precise recording system similar to a banking system must be set up to list the number of tokens received each day. If the students were allowed to keep all of the tokens, many would be lost, some possibly stolen, and the economy itself might collapse; because after a short time, no tokens would be available for continued distribution. Haphazard account of these tokens is quickly recognized by children. Naturally they would rebel since they would not be receiving the due benefits of their efforts. A recording sheet that can be used to list the number of tokens earned by each child was discussed in chapter 3.

Along with the banking system, other recording procedures need to be devised in order to incorporate more precision in the system. Information concerning items purchased, purchase price, and the purchaser should be systematically recorded. From such lists you can learn what items are more desirable to an individual child as well as which items are generally reinforcing for your class as a group. Comparison of these lists to a list of items and prices of things bought can give you a more precise estimate of the amount of money and number of items needed for the store each week.

The store is an extremely important component of the entire token system. It is time consuming and can be tedious, but if conducted properly, the efforts of your work will quickly become apparent.

5. *Collect other necessary materials*

When implementing a token system, many teachers overlook the problem of some type of arrangement for making tokens easy for the children to handle. After a child receives four or more tokens, the problem of the tokens getting lost, falling off the desk, or even simply being played with at inappropriate times arises. Although this problem actually poses no real threat to the system it can become a source of distraction and annoyance for the children, as well as the teacher. Simple provisions can prevent this. For example, provide each child with a box, small bag, or coffee can into which the tokens can be dropped at the time they are received. When chips from Peabody Kits are used as tokens one adequate method is to clip them onto a rubber band worn around the child's wrist or onto a large safety pin attached to the child's clothing.

Not only are the children going to need provisions for tokens, but you also will need some type of aid for carrying the large number of tokens required for dispensation. In order to keep your hands free for other necessary tasks, it would be advisable to wear some type of container on or around your clothing. A few examples are an apron with pockets, a money pouch, an old purse with a shoulder strap or clothing with large pockets. Whatever is most comfortable and accessible should be used.

Any devices such as these that can be used to save time and energy are recommended. However, before including any time and energy-saving devices, be reasonably sure that precision is enhanced and not lost as a result of its inclusion into the system.

6. *Develop a set of rules for your class*

Rules have always been a part of the classroom, whether oral or written, vague and long range, or specific, short range, and behaviorally oriented. It is this last type of rules that should be used in the classroom. Rules should be clear and unambiguous, written so that the children can easily understand the behaviors that are deemed appropriate. They should be specifically stated in measurable terms. An example of a poorly stated classroom rule would be "Practice good citizenship in the classroom." A child may feel he is fulfilling his obligation if he salutes the flag in the morning despite the fact that he kicks the child in front of him. Citizenship undefined is extremely abstract and thus is very difficult to interpret or measure. An example of another type rule to be avoided would be "Don't kick your neighbor." Although this rule focuses on a particular action, is specific, and can be measured, it is negative. Stating the rule in negative terms implies an expectation that the child will display the inappropriate behavior, and it has been shown that children live up to the expectations of adults. A better rule that could be considered in this situation would be "Keep your feet under your own desk when seated." This rule focuses in on one particular action; it is specific, can be measured, and is positive. If the child's feet are anywhere but under his desk, he is breaking the rule. Another advantageous component is that it is unambiguous. It tells the child what is the appropriate behavior to display rather than what is the inappropriate behavior.

The rules developed for the class should provide the basis for determining the behaviors to be reinforced. Only a few rules should be developed in the beginning since it is not feasible to attempt to change a large number of behaviors the first few days, unless you have a great deal of assistance or expertise in the application of behavioral principles. Focus on a small number of behaviors that can be easily handled. When these have been adequately modified move on to a few others. When including additional rules remember to follow the criteria in stating them — make them clear, unambiguous, measurable, and positive.

7. *Determine the specific behaviors of individuals that require modification*

The rules have been set and you are nearly ready to begin. But are you? Being in the field of education you have probably been frequently reminded of the individual differences between human beings. In the classroom, these differences may very well span the physical, social, emotional, and intellectual spectrums. As a result, general rules for the class may not meet the needs of some of the individuals within the group. To meet the needs of each child adequately, their individual characteristics must be taken into account. Rules must be made for specific individuals in order to enhance their growth and to promote a conducive classroom atmosphere. An example might be a child who beats his head on his desk when he is upset. It would not be plausible to develop a rule to modify this inappropriate behavior for the entire class since only one child displays such behavior, but such a behavior that is detrimental to the child should not be ignored. A rule should, therefore, be formulated whereby this particular child can be reinforced when he keeps his head away from his desk (although it is not necessary to reinforce others for the same reason).

Similar to the general rules, you should not initially attempt to modify every behavioral problem of every child in your classroom. Begin with a number that can be easily handled. Change the most severe first and gradually move to others.

8. *Collect information concerning behaviors exhibited related to the rules formulated*

Before an objective judgment of behavioral change can be made we must know what the behavior was like before the attempt to modify it was introduced (baseline). After the rules are made that specify the appropriate behaviors desired, make a list of them. Whenever the opportunity arises tally how many times you see the appropriate behavior being exhibited during a designated time interval. This tally will provide a basis with which to compare later observations after the modification attempts have been incorporated. There will be no need to tell people about the change in your students; you can show them instead. A more detailed explanation of observation methods was included in chapter 3.

9. *Secure help*

By now it has become quite apparent that a program of this nature is time consuming and requires a great deal of concentrated effort, especially in the initial stages. Because of the amount of time required, we believe that outside help should be secured if a full-time teacher's aide is not available. It is true that the program can be carried out alone, but unless you are very familiar with behavioral principles, help is needed.

You may be able to find a volunteer who can assure you that he will be available during the initial stages of the program (approximately ten days). His full-time availability is essential. If for some reason he is not available for training as well as during the time needed for support, another volunteer must be secured and trained, creating a great deal more work for you.

If at all possible, the volunteer should not be a class member's parent or anyone involved with the students since objectivity is a major prerequisite. Any emotional or social involvement with certain members of the class may result in partiality and eventually in the breakdown of the system. All children must have an equal chance to earn tokens based on certain overt behaviors they exhibit. Three possible sources of such volunteers might be civic organizations, college students, or community action groups.

The aide or volunteer must be trained in behavioral principles, the goals you are attempting to achieve, and appropriate ways of reacting to different situations and methods for dispensing tokens. His main jobs will consist of helping in the dispensation of tokens, conducting the store while you work with the remainder of the class, and being available to help individual children with problems they encounter, such as counting tokens, until the children become adept with the system. The most difficult task to learn, which must be stressed in the training process, is the objectivity with which the program needs to be carried out.

When the initial hurdle has been achieved — getting the children hooked on the system — less help will be required and the volunteer can gradually be phased out of the classroom until you are conducting the entire program on your own.

Day-by-Day Procedures

1. *The first day*

The first day you introduce the program into the classroom will be a rewarding venture for you as well as the children. Even before the verbal explanation, excitement will be high on the part of the children as soon as the items for the store are seen.

At the beginning of the day you should set aside time for an explanation of the entire program, including showing the tokens to the children and explaining how they are to be handled at their seats as well as displaying the items for which the tokens can be exchanged. Also included in the explanation should be a discussion of the cost of the items, how the exchange will take place, and above all a discussion of the rules and what is expected in relation to the rules. If a new adult (aide or volunteer) comes into the classroom at this time, he should be introduced and his presence explained. Children cannot be expected to become adequate participants in a game unless they are familiar with the rules and procedures of that game.

At this point distribute to each child a coffee can, rubber band, or any container that will be used to store the tokens earned. Academic activities should be conducted in the standard manner. The only major change from the regular procedure should be the dispensing of tokens for appropriate behavior exhibited. A schedule of continuous reinforcement should be applied so that the children receive a token for every designated appropriate behavior they exhibit. (Although it might be impossible literally to reinforce each child on a continuous schedule, you should come as close as possible.) For some of the problem children you and your aide may have to catch them in the act of exhibiting appropriate behavior. Remember, try to give every child as many tokens as possible so that they can become winners at the game, and thus motivated to win some more — get them hooked.

In the middle of the day the children should be given the opportunity to go to the store. As might be expected it is best to allow only one or two children at the store at one time. This may take a little more time but will eliminate a lot of headaches. Forms should be available at the store regarding items bought, costs, and purchaser. When the children exchange their tokens they should fill in the specified information; if necessary you or the aide can help. Toward the end of the day, store can be held again. A few minutes should be set aside during the first day to observe and record the behaviors designated to be changed. These records can be compared to those taken during baseline as well as to records taken after the first day. In addition to recording behavior, you should take a few moments before the end of the day to collect and record any tokens that the children want to save.

After school discuss with the aide or volunteer the events of the day. Talk about possibilities of more efficient and effective means to conduct various activities, review the rules for appropriateness, and then relax. Your most hectic day of the program will be over.

2.   The second day

The children are already familiar with the system. If they won in the system on the first day, they will be ready to start earning more tokens. Reinforce them for appropriate behavior from the time they enter the room, even before the formal school day begins.

Proceed in the same manner as the first day: following your regular schedule, having the store, recording behavior, and carrying on banking procedures before dismissal. The only major change is one that deals with the store schedule. On day two, hold store only once and schedule it toward the end of the day. In this way, the children will begin to adjust to going a longer period of time before the more basic reinforcers are available.

3.   The third day

Now that things have been going fairly smooth for two days, you will probably tend to relax, but don't. It is approximately at this time that some of the children will begin testing the system. The children know by now that they will be automatically reinforced when they exhibit certain appropriate behaviors, but they will begin wondering if they can fool you and receive tokens without displaying the necessary behaviors. They may even say "You missed me, can I have my token?" This type of behavior is inappropriate and thus should be ignored. Remember, never give a token to a child who asks for one. Be very careful of what you reward. *At this point precision is imperative.* The students may continue testing the system for a week or more, but if consistency is upheld the problem will gradually disappear.

Continue with your schedule; however, delay the time the children can go to the store until the morning of the fourth day, to assist the children in delaying gratification for a longer period of time.

4.   The fourth day

The store should be held in the morning as a carry-over from day three. Procedures should be carried out as usual. As during day three, you should be especially watchful of children going through the testing stages.

5.   The fifth day

The end of the first week is near — a major milestone. On this day, the program should be conducted for the most part as it was during the preceding four days. Store should be held near the close of the day.

A total evaluation of the week's procedures should be considered. From the observations and data obtained, behaviors that have been increased can be noted. Appropriate behaviors that have been radically increased can be reinforced less often and other behaviors you wish to modify can be considered for the next week. Modifications of these newly considered behaviors should not, however, be started until at least the second day of the second week since you will need time to get some baseline data.

From the information gathered concerning the store you can determine those items that appear to be most reinforcing. This information can be the basis for selecting your items for the following week.

6.   *The second week*

Introduce the use of the timer. Remember, explain the procedure to the children. A simple explanation might be, "The timer will be used to help me remember to hand out tokens, since sometimes I get busy and forget to give them out."

Refine your techniques; if anything doesn't appear to be running smoothly, seek a more efficient means of conducting that portion of the program. Store should be held on Wednesday and Friday of the second week.

The program should by now be showing signs of becoming an integral part of your classroom environment. The children, as the most important component of that environment, can begin to have a more influential voice in what takes place. They can begin to be consulted concerning certain aspects of the program. They can have an input as to the items available in the store and make suggestions concerning procedures and rules.

At the end of week two, an evaluation should again be made. Include all recorded information, your subjective evaluation, objective observation data, observations of the volunteer, and the inputs made by the students. Consider these evaluations in planning the strategy to be carried out the following week.

7.   *The third week*

The program should be conducted as it was during the second week with two exceptions. (1) The store should be held only once (last day of week), which should become standard procedure for the remainder of the year. (2) A more complete transition from continuous to intermittent reinforcement should occur. The timer, which was previously discussed, can be set to ring at time periods of various lengths. The range of time lengths is usually from two to twelve minutes, averaging about six minutes. Children who exhibit the specified appropriate behaviors *during* any one interval can be reinforced at the end of that interval.

8.   *The remainder of the year*

The program by now probably has become an integral part of your classroom environment. However, you should not relax. Continued evaluation and refinement must occur if the program is going to remain in operation. Just as the wheels of a machine must be oiled and checked to keep it running at optimal level, so must the components of a token system. If they are allowed to become stagnant, they will disintegrate. Consistency, objectivity, and precision are as important after incorporation as during the initial stages.

Later on in the program, your workload can be somewhat lightened. Certain responsible children may be able to run the store or carry on the banking procedures. This should not, however, occur too quickly; and the choice of students should be as objective as possible. If you continue to read the literature on token systems and are consistent in your evaluations, many more ideas and innovations will occur to you and a very productive year can result.

Evaluation

You may choose to evaluate how well you comprehended the information presented in chapter 4 by responding to the following test items. Cover the answer column with a sheet of paper; then write your answers in the blank spaces provided.

behavior modification token	1. Before actually establishing a token economy you should become familiar with the basic principles of .... as well as with the specifics of .... systems.
observe	2. When tokens are dispensed for appropriate behavior the teacher must place himself in a position to .... as much behavior as possible.
classroom (or setting)	3. The .... must be arranged to permit you to reinforce appropriate behavior immediately.
Tokens	4. .... should not be easy to duplicate.
100	5. When considering the number of tokens that will be needed, you should estimate approximately .... tokens for each child.
desirable	6. The more .... the items included in the store, the harder the children will work to obtain them.
inexpensive	7. In the beginning, many .... items should be available in the store so the

children will not have to wait to start winning in the system.

store
later

8. Initially, the .... should be held quite often, while in the .... stages more time can elapse.

tokens

9. The children as well as the teacher will need containers to keep their .... in.

behavior

10. Rules should be written so that the children can easily understand the .... that is deemed appropriate.

rules

11. In some instances,.............must be made for specific individuals in order to enhance their growth.

help

12. Before establishing a token economy it would probably be advisable to obtain ....

explanation

13. At the beginning of the first day you should set aside time for a/an .... of the entire program.

catch

14. Try to .... some of the problem children in the act of exhibiting appropriate behavior.

test
consistency

15. The students may try to .... the system, but if .... is maintained the problem will gradually disappear.

evaluation

16. To have an effective program contin-ued .... and refinement must occur.

5

Procedures for
Teaching
Teachers

The training of teachers to be effective educators is a monumental task, to say the least. There is no universal agreement as to *what* to teach teachers about effective teaching, let alone *how* to teach teachers to be effective. We believe all teachers should know how to set up a token system, and we have tried to give step-by-step procedures to follow for developing a token economy; yet we would be the first to admit the materials, ideas, and suggestions contained herein are inadequate. To find out where we go from here, we have looked to other professions to give us some suggestions that may help us better prepare teachers.

Several years before he got involved in the profession of education, one of the authors traveled for a brief period of time as a magician. During this time of nomadism, he became acquainted with the techniques and training of fellow magicians, illusionists, hypnotists, and night-club performers. Of all the performers, the mind readers were the most interesting and intriguing. However, as he became familiar with the basic skills necessary to be an effective mind reader, his interest and intrigue turned to appreciation and admiration. Skilled mind readers fascinate most everyone, including fellow mind readers, because instead of relying upon illusions, sleight of hand, or gimmicks, they rely primarily upon a scientific approach to human behavior based on a careful history of data collection. Most people do not understand or appreciate the training involved in mind reading. This chapter will describe one of the most widely distributed mind-reading acts ever published (Read, 1945) and discuss its relevancy to teacher training and specifically apply it to the teaching of a token economy.*

Possibly the best and most efficient way to describe and explain the workings of this mind reading act is to quote its distributor (Kanter, 1950):

> The act requires two people (performer and the medium). The spectators are requested to merely think of any questions they wish answered. The medium may be genuinely blindfolded, and remains on the stage. The performer steps down among the spectators, and from that moment he never speaks a word to the medium during the entire performance. A spectator whispers his question in the performer's ear, the spectator raises his hand for identification and requests the medium to "Please answer my question." The medium instantly responds, giving the intimate details as to the person, or persons, articles, dates, places, etc., involved. . . .
>
> This [the question] is acknowledged, whereupon the performer locates the next questioner who raises his hand and repeats the simple request, "Please answer my question," and thus the performance continues in snappy fashion without waits or interruptions from start to finish (p. 390).

This system is of course a highly complex and technical system of codes. How the codes are conveyed from performer to medium is not germane to teacher training; however, how the medium knows what question is being asked and what all this has to do with education and teacher training are important questions which can best be answered by turning to the original source (Read, 1945).

> While thousands of questions may be propounded, an analysis reveals the fact that all of them may be "boiled down" to about a hundred or so. People in general are not aware of this, having never given it a thought. It means nothing to them, but it is of vital importance in an act of this kind. Our system doesn't have to handle very much in order to cover practically everything that will be asked (p. 5).

Seemingly what has happened is that the mind-reading profession has taken complex human behavior, analyzed it, categorized it, classified it,

---

*This comparison of mind reading to teaching was adapted from: Payne, J. S. "Similarities of procedures for teaching teachers and teaching mind readers." *Phi Delta Kappan* (1972), *53*, 375-76.

and used it to do the seemingly impossible. They didn't quit or give up because of individual differences, social or group dynamics, large subject - medium ratio, poor facilities, or multiracial complexities. Rather, they took all these differences, all this conglomeration of data and boiled it down to 110 questions; and better yet, they came up with answers to these questions.

We must teach to the individual child. While we recognize the com-plexity of human behavior as well as the many dangers of cookbook ap-proaches to education, we are aware that educational procedures are imprecise and that the educational process itself has gone through periods of revolution and, unfortunately, not evolution. In education we have not accumulated knowledge building fact upon fact as have the physical sciences, biological sciences or the spiritual world. Education must be concerned about probabilities, not plausabilities or absolutes. How probable is it that a specific event will happen in a specific situation?

In a night club mind-reading act we know that it is highly probable that certain types of questions will be asked at the 6:00 p.m. performance that will differ from the 8:00 p.m., 10:00 p.m., or 12:00 p.m. performances. In education we know that when children play on a playground made up of gravel someone someday is going to throw rocks. We know this as ex-perienced educators, but what teacher has ever been instructed to an-ticipate this situation, let alone handle it — and know alternatives for handling the problem. The lesson we can learn from the mind-reading profession is the value of keeping records of children's behavior and the compilation of alternatives for dealing with the specific behaviors.

Each year young bright dynamic teachers enter the teaching profession who later become discouraged because they were inadequately prepared and unwarned of possible problem situations that could have been an-ticipated. Most teachers are taught that you can't predict human behavior because you are involved with individual students, with individual teachers who have individual personalities in individual situations. Teachers are indoctrinated on this individualization principle, yet each year public school officials witness the same inadequate techniques handed down from generation to generation — the *same techniques* used by individual teachers with individual children in individual situations. These include such techniques and procedures as:

"Write, 'I will not chew gum in school' 100 times."

"Stay after school."

"Go to the principal's office."

"Sit in the corner."

"Just for that, no recess."

"Just for that, no gym class."

"If you don't straighten up, I'll write a note to your mother."

"Clean the erasers or chalkboard or wash the desks or sweep the floor..."

So in this individualized world in education unfortunately we have taught the fictitious "normal" child using the same techniques and procedures. To illustrate typical techniques used by teachers and to recommend additional alternatives we wish to present to teachers the *Rule of 5, the First Two Don't Count.*

1. Ignore

   Many times when a teacher is involved in a problem situation, the first temptation is to ignore the behavior being exhibited.

2. Punish

   There are four types of commonly used punishment.

   a. Contact (child is struck)
   b. Chew (child is verbally attacked)
   c. Deprive (child is deprived of an activity like recess)
   d. Remove (child is removed from the situation; e.g., dropped from school or sent to the principal's office)

Ignoring and punishing are the two most common practices used by teachers when confronted with problems; yet the three alternatives remaining (almost any alternatives) may eventually separate the professional education technician from the lay person. The three remaining procedures will differ from situation to situation; but if individualized instruction is to become a reality, new procedures and techniques must be developed and the first two techniques need to be either eliminated, minimally used, or used with discretion. Ignoring and/or punishing specific behaviors can be effective in many cases with many different behaviors (as mentioned in the previous chapters), but they do not work all the time with all behaviors nor are they necessarily the most effective means of dealing with most behaviors, especially when used singularly. Because records have not been kept by educators throughout the years, it is difficult to determine alternative methods for handling various situations. Let's take a look at the rock-throwing problems. If we follow the *Rule of 5, the First Two Don't Count*, we cannot ignore the child, we cannot hit or punish the child, we cannot verbally yell or scream at the child, we cannot deprive the child of an activity such as gym class, and lastly we cannot send the child to the principal's office or send him home. What is left to do? Let's stretch our minds and think of some alternatives. We could structure the environment and asphalt the playground. This may be somewhat expensive, but it would minimize rock throwing. We could develop an exciting recess activity that would keep the child busy so he would neither want nor have time to throw rocks. We could place the child's throwing arm in a sling or require him to keep his hand in his pocket for one recess or wear a glove on his throwing hand to remind him not to throw rocks or tie his throwing hand to his leg or...or...or. Just a plain old discussion or comment is also sometimes very effective. Now if the child is involved in a class situation using a token system, *many other alternatives are available* to the teacher; i.e., he may issue tokens to children not throwing rocks, he may issue tokens to the child in question at times when he is engaged in non-rock-throwing activities, he may ask the class what to do about the situation (past experience tells us his peers will usually suggest a certain number of tokens be taken away as a means of punishment). The alternatives could go on into infinity depending on the resources and creativity of the teacher.

Although in our opinion the use of a token system provides a teacher with more opportunities for increasing feasible and effective alternatives for handling classroom situations, the crucial and possibly the most important stage in teacher training is to collect some records of problem situations so we will know what the problems are, have been, and will be. Earlier we presented answers to questions that were commonly asked pertaining to establishing, developing, and implementing a token economy. We are now ready to collect, record, analyze, categorize, and classify problem situations recorded by educators implementing the token system.

We ask that as you encounter problems or even as you solve problems you forward these to us for compilation and future dissemination. In this way we, like mind readers, can intelligently begin the training and preparation of professionals in the analysis of human behavior. Just fill out the form on page 55 and forward it to us as you encounter a problem. We are interested in the problems and we're interested in solutions as well as unsuccessful attempts to solve the problems.

In summary, we are concerned about two basic things: (1) the necessity of recording, analyzing, categorizing, and classifying problem situations by educators using a token economy and (2) the developing of creative and effective alternatives for handling problem situations. Although this procedure may lead to the danger of a cookbookish approach, this may be a place to start in assisting and equipping new teachers for the educational battlefield or playground, whichever the case may be.

References

Kanter, M. *Kanter's catalog of magic, №o. 9.* Philadelphia, 1950, p. 390.

Read, R. W. *The Calostro mind reading act.* Closter, N.J.: Calostro Publications, 1945, pp. 3-5.

Name:

Address:

School:

Send problem situations to:
    Dr. James S. Payne
    Peabody Hall
    University of Virginia
    Charlottesville, Virginia 22903

The problem situation is as follows (be specific, concise, and objective):

Unsuccessful attempt(s) to solve the problem (include specific failure reactions to your attempt to solve the problem):

Successful attempt(s) to solve the problem:

6

Limitations of
Behavior
Modification:
Fact or Fallacy?

Discussions concerning the limitations of any new idea or system are inevitable. Recently articles about the limitations of behavior modification have begun to appear in psychological and educational literature. Drawbacks that attack the theoretical schema and premises of behavior modification as well as its plausibility in practical situations have been brought forth. This chapter discusses a few of the most commonly cited limitations along with our perceptions as to the fact or fallacy of these limitations.

Potential for Misuse

Wood (1968) expressed concern that behavior modification is a powerful tool that has potential for misuse. We share this concern. Examples of misuse include:

1. A behavior chosen for acceleration may not only be of no real benefit to the child but may actually be detrimental to his progress. A common example is when a six-year-old child hears his younger brother speaking in an infantile manner and observes him receiving his mother's attention as a result. The six-year-old may try baby talk in an attempt to receive mother's attention. If adults reinforce this behavior, thinking it is cute, by laughing or providing attention for the action, the behavior will increase in frequency and may hinder the child's speech development. When reinforcement procedures are applied to such detrimental behaviors in an even more precise manner, as in a planned behavior modification program, the acceleration will occur more rapidly, hindering the child's progress to a greater extent.

   If one child, as in our illustration, exhibits a distracting behavior that has been accelerated by an adult's or peer's attention, not even considering the long-range consequences for the child, it can be annoying. However, when a group of children exhibit such behaviors, the teacher may be faced with mass bedlam. It is, therefore, imperative that the teacher use behavioral principles with discretion and foresight.

2. Often, especially in a disruptive classroom, when a teacher discovers a method that enables him to get the children to work on academic activities, he may go overboard and not provide time for other nonacademic activities. He fails to recognize that children are people, with an even shorter attention span than adults. They too desire and need a break from a sometimes grueling academic schedule. Rest periods and play activities should be an integral part of any classroom schedule. Behavior modification is a tool that can be employed to modify behavior and should be used in conjunction with an adequate and well balanced daily schedule.

3. Such a powerful system may cause dictatorial tendencies to reveal themselves. If applied precisely, a teacher can make children do almost anything he desires. However, we have faith in the great majority of teachers and feel that they put foremost in their thoughts the needs of their students rather than their own wants and needs. Since behavior modification is an extremely powerful tool, the productive development of students should and must remain the primary concern of any teacher operating a token economy.

In sum we would say that the fault does not lie *within* the system; the onus is on the *manager* of the system who misuses it.

It's a bribe

In an article about paying children for school achievement, Green and Stachnik (1968) stated:

Critics of such a system would undoubtedly accuse schools of "bribing" the children. The charge is invalid. "To bribe," according to Webster's Seventh New Collegiate Dictionary, means "money or favor bestowed on or promised to a person in a position of trust to pervert his judgment or corrupt his conduct." That hardly describes what the schools would be doing. The goal could in fact be quite the opposite — the strengthening of behaviors which would one day make it possible for the child to become a productive member of society. This is the same set of rules to which we have all long been accustomed. We received a high grade in school when we studied and achieved, a low grade when we did not; as children, we were praised for being "good" and reproached when we were "bad." We are paid a specified amount of money for a specified amount of work. How many of us would continue to report for work if told there would be no more paychecks? (p. 229)

Limited in Scope

Behavior modification procedures rely on extrinsic motivation. MacMillan and Forness (1970) stated that behavior modification is limited in scope in that it does not make use of many intrinsic motivators. We recognize that such motivators as a child's need for a sense of competence in the activity in which he is engaging, as discussed by White (1965), and Festinger's (1957) recognition of curiosity as a result of cognitive incongruencies are not accounted for in the behavior modification model. These motivators are not included in the model because they are abstract and can not be precisely observed and measured. There are many theories which attempt to explain human behavior, but teachers are on the firing line and need something that has been found *through applied classroom research* to motivate children, something that they (teachers) can observe, measure, and *control*.

Another part of this argument is that behavior modification thwarts the creativity and self-expression of the child. If a teacher doesn't consider such development important, he may tend to inhibit the development of these characteristics. A class full of unthinking robots may evolve, but this would be a result of the teacher's attitude. It is in no way a result of the system itself. A teacher who places great importance on creativity and self-expression can use behavior modification techniques to maximize such potentials. For example, immediate, extrinsic reinforcement can be provided after a child verbally states several different ways a pencil can be used.

Narrow in Focus

Another argument says that since behavior modification concentrates on observable behavior, it does not use the child's cumulative folder, test data, etc. to help design a total educational program for him. In answer to this charge, Hewett (1968), when discussing the use of behavior modification with a boy named Billy, wrote:

> This approach does not by any means preclude consideration of Billy's interpersonal, emotional, sensory, and neurological problems in the selection of appropriate tasks to assign him. Those situations producing withdrawal or anxiety initially will be avoided. Tasks which demand visual, auditory, or motor skills which Billy does not possess will not be given him. Previous school records, case study information, and diagnostic test information will all be utilized in the development of a suitable program for Billy in the classroom (p. 35).

Not Goal Oriented

Hewett, Taylor, and Artuso (1969) said:

> The powerful methodology of the behavior modification approach is not matched by concern with goals for learning. . . . It is this lack of balanced emphasis on goals and methods that may preclude the appliance of behavior modification in the field of education, particularly in the public schools, and thereby may greatly limit its usefulness (p. 523).

If a theory such as Piaget's developmental theory is helpful to a teacher when attempting to determine goals, it can be used. Afterwards a behavior modification approach can be applied when attempting to reach the goals established. This, in essence, is what Hewett and his associates did in the Santa Monica Project (1968). They used a developmental sequence of educational goals postulated by Hewett (1968) to assess children in terms of their developmental learning deficiencies and establish goals. Afterwards, as a part of their engineered classroom design, they applied behavior modification techniques to reach the goals established.

As we have implied throughout this book, behavior modification is not a panacea for all of education's ills. It is a tool that can be utilized to modify behavior. No reputable behavior modification specialist has, to our knowledge, ever claimed that behavior modification, in theory or use, guides the teacher in the establishment of worthwhile goals. However, this does not limit its usefulness as a tool to modify academic and social behaviors toward such goals. Behavior modification provides an excellent means of achieving already established goals.

A Token Reinforcement Plan Is Inflexible

As Haring and Phillips (1972) stated:

> Token reinforcement may be the most flexible reinforcement plan to adopt in the classroom. It not only allows for the individual needs of all the children but also provides a system whereby satiation and deprivation are best controlled. If the child is given time only for extra gym or extra

art after responding appropriately, he will soon be satiated by these reinforcers, even if the events themselves are reinforcing for a time. If token reinforcement is used, however, and diverse opportunities can be paid for with tokens, the child can choose what he would like to do at the moment rather than engage only in a specified event (p. 69).

Costly to Operate

Many teachers, especially those not familiar with the operation of behavior modification programs, worry that the cost of such a program in money, teacher time, and class time is too great to warrant its use.

Monetary cost was discussed in chapter 3 and only a brief review of what was said at that time will be included here. Money can possibly be obtained from groups such as concerned civic groups. The use of free merchandise, rental items, and free activity time can considerably defray the cost of the basic reinforcers.

The implementation of a successful behavior modification program is costly in teacher time and class time, but when compared with wasted time in a disruptive classroom, the cost is minimal. In the initial stages a great deal of time is consumed in the implementation of the system. But after the program becomes an integral part of the classroom setting, the time required of the teacher may be considerably less than that which is required to handle discipline problems. The cost in class time for the program is generally less than the amount of time wasted when handling discipline problems.

Since the utmost consideration of the teacher should be the progress of his students, the efficiency and effectiveness of this method properly utilized cannot be overrated. It is, therefore, the place of the teacher to make the judgment which is more important — the amount of time and money or the progress of his students.

Ignores Development of Self-Esteem

In answer to this contention, Krumboltz and Krumboltz (1972) wrote:

> How do you develop a child's self-esteem? You make sure that he is learning to master the tasks in his environment, that he is praised and rewarded for his accomplishments and assured that he is loved and respected by those around him. The end result of these behaviors is the development of a feeling in a child which we label "self-esteem."
>
> The evidence is quite clear that the pattern of reinforcement provided by teachers and parents can produce or destroy self-esteem. An adult who punishes unsatisfactory behavior but ignores good behavior tends to develop a child with a fear of failure. An adult who rewards satisfactory behavior but ignores unsatisfactory behavior helps a child develop a positive attitude toward achievement (pp. 248-49).

Not Effective for All Children

Some children do not profit when working under a behavior modification program. This is a common argument set forth by opposing theorists as well as some teachers. However, a basic premise of behavior modification is that every human being desires something and is willing to perform in such a way as to achieve that something that is desired. If this premise is true, there is no one with whom this approach will not work. The problem arises when ineffective reinforcers are used or goals are set too high. Deprivation is usually the basis under which a reinforcer takes on motivating characteristics. If a child is satiated with candy and toys at home, he is not likely to find them effective reinforcers in the classroom. He may, however, find the use of a tape recorder, which allows him to hear his own voice, attractive. For this child, therefore, the renting of a tape recorder for short periods during the day may be a successful basic reinforcer. Discovering appropriate reinforcers can be difficult. But through careful observation and discussions with each child, a desirable motivator can be found; and if it is found, the child will perform. As we have said, the desirability of the reinforcer to the child to a great extent determines the effectiveness of the program.

Some children will test the system. If they win the teacher may say the system is ineffective with these particular children. Again this should be viewed as a limitation on the part of the teacher and not the system. The precision and consistency of the system may be tested, for example, by children attempting to obtain reinforcers (tokens, checkmarks, or attention) without performing the appropriate behaviors or even refusing reinforcement to get a reaction from the teacher. However, if consistency is maintained, this testing period will soon pass. If the teacher is inconsistent or reacts to the test, the breakdown of the system may be forthcoming.

Behavior Modification Advocates Forget to Make Assignments Exciting

We would like to make it perfectly clear that progressive education/open classroom advocates do *not* have a corner on the market when it comes to advocating the making of assignments interesting, exciting, and relevant. We have long advocated making learning as relevant and as enjoyable as humanly possible. We like to see teachers set up learning centers, utilize community resources, and allow children freedom to move, to express their own opinions, and disagree with the teacher. However, children can learn to move freely about the class or to disagree with each other and the teacher in a responsible manner. Teachers are employed to teach; it is their job to teach children appropriate social and academic behavior — for example, to express their opinions intelligently and responsibly.

If the teacher makes the physical appearance of the classroom as attractive as possible, provides exciting things for the children to do, *and provides rewards for accomplishments*, the classroom will very likely be a place children will enjoy being. Without an opportunity to earn rewards, the classroom, in our opinion, would be a little less enjoyable place to be. The logic of this seems compelling.

Focuses on Social Behaviors rather than Academic Learning

Critics unfamiliar with behavior modification often say that modification of a child's social behaviors does not mean that academic learning will be fostered, and academic learning is the main reason the child is in school. But behavior modification is only a tool to modify behavior, *academic or social*; how it is used, for what, and when, depends on the teacher. It is true, however, that the first behaviors that are modified are often students' social behaviors. Modification of these behaviors usually occurs first in order to develop a setting conducive to the acquisition of academic knowledge. A child can not be expected to attend to an academic task if he is being hit by another student or the child behind him is discussing a party to be held the following weekend. Unnecessary distractions need to be held to a minimum. Then efficient learning at least has a chance to take place. When disruptive behaviors have been modified so that a conducive learning atmosphere exists, behavior modification techniques can be employed to enhance academic learning.

Does Not Deal with the Underlying Causes of Maladaptive Behavior

Whelan and Haring (1966) have discussed the facts concerning this limitation.

While behavioral modification is not antagonistic to any professional concerned with such problems, an individual more concerned with unconscious behavioral determinants might claim that removing inappropriate behaviors is merely changing the surface signs of emotional disorders. This individual might also assert that the underlying conflicts which caused the behavior have not been resolved; therefore, the individual will merely substitute other, and possibly more, deviant behaviors. A review of cases where behavioral modification techniques have been applied to removal of deviant behaviors indicates that effort "directed at elimination of maladapted behavior ('symptoms') is successful and long lasting" (Grossberg, 1964, p. 83) (p. 288).

Krumboltz and Krumboltz (1972) were asked, "Isn't it necessary for a person to be aware of the underlying reasons for his own behavior to change it?" They answered:

No. People frequently change their behavior without being aware of the "reason." Furthermore, people can give elaborate verbal explanations for the origins of their inappropriate behavior and still continue to engage in it. The elaborate explanation of "causes" may serve as justification of the behavior and excuses them from any effort to improve. The idea that "insight" is necessary for change is a Freudian notion which has misled psychiatrists and psychologists for years. Some kinds of insights may be useful but are not essential for change (pp. 240-41).

Conclusion

The limitations reviewed in this chapter are indeed plausible ones. It is, however, our position that the majority are attributable to the shortcomings of the user, rather than the system itself. One major limitation attributable to the system itself is the cost. However, the expenditure in time and money is worthwhile when the results that can be achieved are considered.

References

Festinger, L. A. *A theory of cognitive dissonance.* Evanston, Ill.: Row, Peterson, 1957.

Green, R. L. and T. J. Stachnik. *"Money, motivation, and academic achievement." Phi Delta Kappan* (1968), *50,* 228-30.

Haring, N. G. and E. L. Phillips. *Analysis and modification of classroom behavior.* Englewood Cliffs, N.J.: Prentice-Hall, Inc., 1972.

Hewett, F. M. *The emotionally disturbed child in the classroom.* Boston: Allyn & Bacon, Inc., 1968.

Hewett, F. M., F. D. Taylor, and A. A. Artuso. *"The Santa Monica Project: Evaluation of an engineered classroom design with emotionally disturbed children." Exceptional Children* (1969), *35,* 523-29.

Krumboltz, J. D. and H. B. Krumboltz. *Changing children's behavior.* Englewood Cliffs, N.J.: Prentice-Hall, Inc., 1972.

MacMillan, D. L. and S. R. Forness. "Behavior modification: Limitation and liabilities." *Exceptional Children* (1970), *37,* 291-97.

Whelan, R. E and N. Haring. "Modification and maintenance of behavior through systematic application of consequences." *Exceptional Children* (1966), *32,* 281-89.

White, R. W. "Motivation reconsidered: The concept of competence." In I. J. Gordon (ed.), *Human development: Readings in research.* Glenview, Ill.: Scott, Foresman and Company, 1965.

Wood, F. H. "Behavior modification techniques in context." *Newsletter of the Council for Children with Behavior Disorders* (1968), 5(4), 12-15.

7

Articles,
Books and Films

Token reinforcement is a powerful tool that can be employed to hinder as well as to foster academic and social growth. Wood (1968) stated that "like many 'tools', behavior modification techniques are themselves morally blind. Like a stout sword, they work equally well in the hands of hero or tyrant" (p. 14). We feel that the overwhelming majority of teachers would not intentionally employ reinforcement techniques to hinder the progress of a child. However, token reinforcement can be *un*intentionally misapplied to the detriment of children.

Token systems can also be misrepresented. One day one of the authors overheard a teacher say that she had employed a "token reinforcement system" in her classroom and it failed. When questioned, she revealed that she had given out two or three tokens without any back-up reinforcers for which the children could exchange their tokens. If you have read the first six chapters of this book, you know very well why the "token system" she employed was unsuccessful.

It is imperative that any teacher contemplating the establishment of a token system become very familiar with behavior modification principles and techniques. This chapter is intended to provide a comprehensive, although not exhaustive, list of abstracts or descriptions of articles, books, and films in the area of behavior modification. Read the chapter; for a more indepth understanding of behavior modification, we encourage you to study in their original form the ones that are of interest to you.

We have included those articles, books, and films that were felt to be most informative to a teacher contemplating the establishment of a token economy. Research studies are reviewed first. Each one is abstracted. An attempt was made to avoid including highly technical research. Books and descriptive reports are reviewed next. The contents of these writings are described and/or summarized. Finally, the contents of several films on behavior modification are described.

Research Studies

Andrews, J. K. "The results of a pilot program to train teachers in the classroom application of behavior modification techniques." *Journal of School Psychology* (1970), *8*, 37-42.

Purpose.   The purpose of the project was to study the feasibility of a short-term teacher-training program in the classroom application of behavior modification techniques.

Subjects.   Eleven teachers of kindergarten through grade four participated in the project. They ranged in experience from one to ten years. With the exception of two teachers of the educable mentally retarded, one teacher of the trainable mentally retarded, and one speech therapist, all the teachers were regular class teachers.

Procedure.   Four one and one-half hour training sessions were held. *Living with Children* by Patterson and Gullion (1968) was used as the text. Lectures and discussions during the four sessions centered around such topics as observing and recording behavior, reinforcement principles, and extinction. During the final session the teachers were asked to complete a course evaluation questionnaire.

Results.   Data obtained on several children enrolled in the classrooms of the teachers participating in the project and responses to the questionnaires tended to indicate that a short-term teacher-training program in behavior modification can result in student as well as teacher behavior change.

Becker, W.C., C.H. Madsen, C.R. Arnold, and D.R. Thomas. "The contingent use of teacher attention and praise in reducing classroom behavior problems." *The Journal of Special Education* (1967), *1*, 287-307.

Purpose. The purposes of the five studies reported in this article were to demonstrate how the contingent use of teacher attention and praise can be applied in managing behavior problems in elementary classrooms and to explore ways of training teachers to be more effective in their use of praise and attention.

Subjects. The subjects were ten children (C. A. [chronological age], 6-8 to 10-6; I. Q., 73 to 97) enrolled in five different classrooms in an elementary school in Urbana, Illinois.

Procedure. Baseline data were recorded for a five-week period and then the experimental program was implemented for nine weeks. The five teachers involved in the studies were given rules to follow for classroom management such as make explicit rules as to what is expected, ignore behaviors which interfere with learning and give praise and attention for appropriate behaviors.

Results and Conclusion:

The average "deviant" behavior for ten children in five classes was 62.13 percent during baseline and 29.19 percent during the experimental period. The t-test for the differences between correlated means was significant well beyond the .001 level. All children showed less deviant behavior during the experimental phase...

The results of these investigations demonstrate that quite different kinds of teachers can learn to apply behavioral principles effectively to modify the behavior of problem children (p. 306).

Comment. In addition to the data being analyzed for the children as a group, the data were also analyzed separately for each child. Descriptions of each child and his teachers were also included.

Birnbrauer, J.S., M.M. Wolf, J.J. Kidder, and C.E. Tague. "Classroom behavior of retarded pupils with token reinforcement." *Journal of Experimental Child Psychology* (1965), *2*, 219-35.

Purpose. The study was undertaken to ascertain the effects of withdrawing a token reinforcement system for a relatively long period and subsequently reinstating it.

Subjects. Seventeen students enrolled to a programmed learning classroom at Rainer School participated in the study. The students were mildly or moderately retarded (C. A., 8 to 14 yrs., I. Q., 50 to 72). They were selected for this particular class because their performance was at a first grade level or below in academic achievement in spite of up to 5 years of previous education at Rainer School.

Design.   A within-group design was used. Data were collected during three conditions: baseline or token reinforcement ($B1$), experimental or no token reinforcement (NT), and return to baseline ($B2$).

Procedure.   During $B1$ and $B2$ the following events occurred: (1) tokens and social approval were given for correct responses to instructional materials and cooperative behavior; (2) when incorrect responses and inappropriate, but not disruptive, behavior were exhibited the teacher simply ignored the behavior; and (3) when disruptive behavior was displayed, a brief time-out period immediately followed. During NT, tokens were not dispensed; however, approval for appropriate behavior and the employment of time-out sessions were the same as in $B1$ and $B2$.

Daily records were kept on the amount of time spent in time-out (measure of disruptive behavior). Data were also kept on percentage of errors (accuracy) and number of items completed on the academic programs (productivity).

Results.

> Although each pupil reacted to the removal and reinstatement of token reinforcement in a somewhat idiosyncratic way, three general patterns were obtained. (1) Five Ss [subjects] showed, for all practical purposes, no adverse effects of NT. (2) Six Ss increased in percentage of errors in NT, but continued to cooperate and to complete the same or a greater number of items. (3) Four Ss increased in percentage of errors, accomplished less work, and became serious disciplinary problems during NT. After tokens were reinstated, most of the Ss completed progressively more work and stabilized at levels of percentage of errors that were lower than at any previous time (p. 225).

Broden, M., R. V. Hall, A. Dunlap, and R. Clark, "Effects of teacher attention and a token reinforcement system in a junior high school special education class." *Exceptional Children* (1970), *36*, 341-49.

Purpose.   The purposes of this study were to investigate the influence of teacher attention and token reinforcement on disruptive behavior of students enrolled in a junior high school special education class.

Subjects.   Eight boys and five girls served as subjects. All subjects were performing several years below grade equivalent in at least one major academic area and had additional problems such as reading deficits, emotional instability, and incoherent speech.

Setting.   The study was conducted in a junior high school special education class taught by a first-year teacher.

Procedure. Data regarding fifth period study and nonstudy behavior were collected under the following conditions. (1) The teacher was requested to conduct class in her usual manner and to ignore the observer. (2) The teacher was asked to give attention to study behavior only and to ignore all nonstudying. (3) A kitchen timer was set to go off at random intervals averaging eight minutes. Students who were in their seats and quiet when the timer sounded earned a mark on a card taped to their desk. Students were allowed to leave for lunch one minute earlier for each mark earned. (4) The timer and early dismissal contingency was removed and only social reinforcement for study was given. (5) The teacher attended to nonstudy behavior and ignored study behavior. (6) The teacher again attended to study behavior and ignored nonstudy behavior. (7) Timer and early dismissal for lunch were reinstated. (8) The timer was discontinued and the pupils were put on a token point system. Points earned could be exchanged for classroom privileges such as early dismissal for lunch, getting a drink, or sharpening a pencil. (9) Postchecks were taken in the classroom for a month and a half when the teacher was not instructed to conduct her class in any particular manner. In addition to data being taken during fifth period, data were collected during all periods of the day under baseline (condition 1 above), token point system, reversal to baseline, reinstatement of token point system, and postcheck conditions.

Results. The token point system was found to reduce disruptive behavior more effectively than any of the other conditions including teacher attention.

Comment. This study would tend to indicate that token reinforcement is more powerful than social reinforcement when initially attempting to reduce disruptive behaviors of students.

Coleman, R. "A pilot demonstration of the utility of reinforcement techniques in trainable programs." *Education and Training of the Mentally Retarded (1970),* 5, 68-70.

Purpose. The purpose of the investigation was to determine the effectiveness of utilizing reinforcement techniques to enhance the counting achievement of a trainable mentally retarded (TMR) child in a public school setting.

Subject. The subject was an eight-year-old boy with a Stanford Binet I. Q. of 40.

Procedure. The experimenter worked with the subject on an individual basis for ten minutes each day for thirteen days. Fifteen numbered square wooden blocks were used as materials. The blocks were arranged in random order on a table. The subject was asked to put a certain numbered block in the experimenter's hand. The number of the block requested varied.

Candy was given for primary reinforcement. Secondary reinforcers (verbal praise) also accompanied the subject's successes. In the beginning of each session a continuous schedule was employed. However, toward the end of each session a mixed schedule was used; that is, the subject sometimes received reinforcement for each success and at other times for every other success.

Result. The Wide Range Achievement Test, Brenner Development Gestalt Test of School Readiness, and an adapted number concepts task from the Stanford-Binet were administered before and after treatment. There was a demonstrated increase in counting ability shown by pre- and post-test results.

Gardner, J.M., D.J. Brust, and L.S. Watson, "A scale to measure skill in applying modification techniques to the mentally retarded." *American Journal of Mental Deficiency* (1970), *74*, 633-36.

Purpose. The study was undertaken to develop a scale to measure effectiveness in applying behavior modification techniques to the treatment of the mentally retarded.

Subjects. A group of twenty attendants enrolled in a behavior modification inservice training program at Columbus State Institute were used as a pool from which subjects were drawn. The number of subjects used at any one time varied throughout the different phases of the study. All subjects were female and ranged from 18 to 40 in chronological age. The mean educational level was the 11th grade. All the subjects were working with severely and profoundly retarded residents of Columbus State Institute (Ohio) and had been employed for less than six months.

Procedure. A scale for measuring skill in applying behavior modification techniques in the classroom was developed. In order to develop the scale, "behavior modification skills" were broken down into four component parts. Items corresponding to each of these components were constructed. Shaping, communicating, establishing rapport, and reinforcing were the four major components identified.

A role-playing procedure with two trainers alternately assuming the role of patient and trainer was used along with other procedures to provide an opportunity to use the scale. As a result its reliability and validity could be investigated. The job of the trainer in these role playing sessions was to train the patient in self-care skills and to obey simple verbal commands.

Results:

> Interscorer, split-half, and test-retest reliability were all high. Scores on the rating scale were found to correspond to global evaluations of training proficiency and correlated highly with a test of principles of behavior modification. (p.633).

Comments. We recommend that you read, study, and think about this article. An effective means of evaluating a person's skill in applying behavior modification techniques would be an invaluable tool to possess.

Grieger, R. N. "Behavior modification with a total class: A case report." *Journal of School Psychology* (1970), *8*, 103-6.

Purpose. The two major purposes of this study were to demonstrate the usefulness of reinforcement principles with a total class and to demonstrate the feasibility of using teachers to establish and operate a reinforcement program.

Subjects. Nine children enrolled in a "semi-self-contained" primary class served as subjects. The class was located in a school operated to provide educational and psychological services to children with perceptual-motor based and/or emotional based learning disabilities. The children ranged in age from 7-11 to 11-3, with a mean age of 9-3. All the children were achieving at least one grade below expectation, although they were all of average intelligence.

Procedure. Four rude behaviors exhibited by the children enrolled were pinpointed. These were: hitting, making spraying noises, name calling, and calling out without permission. Baseline data on the number of times these behaviors occurred was recorded and a reinforcement program was then devised. A combination social, object, and token reward system was used. The entire school day was scheduled into a series of ten-minute periods. Candy was given to any child who during each period (1) refrained from hitting or pushing another child, (2) made no spraying noise, (3) refrained from name calling and (4) did not call out without permission more than two times. The teacher ignored any inappropriate behaviors displayed and attended to a child only when he raised his hand.

By the second week of the four weeks of the study the periods were lengthened to twenty-five minutes. Later in the program, chips could be exchanged for desirable items.

Results. The four behaviors decreased in frequency substantially after the implementation of the behavior modification program.

Comment. One should be careful in interpreting the results of this study since there was no return to baseline and then a reinstatement of the program. Nevertheless, the study seems to demonstrate that reinforcement programs can be implemented successfully by teachers for a total class.

Hewett, F., F. Taylor, and A. Artuso. "The Santa Monica project: Evaluation of an engineered classroom design with emotionally disturbed children." *Exceptional Children* (1969), *35*, 523-29.

Purpose. The purpose of the investigation was to determine the effectiveness of an engineered classroom design in maintaining student attention to tasks and in enhancing reading and arithmetic achievement scores.

Subject.   The subjects were 54 emotionally disturbed pupils ranging in chronological age from 8-10 to 11-11 and in measured intelligence from 85 to 113, as determined by the WISC (Wechsler Intelligence Scale for Children).

Procedure.   Subjects were assigned to experimental and control groups in such a way as to arrive at matched class groupings with respect to I.Q., age, and reading and arithmetic achievement. Teachers in the experimental groups were instructed to utilize the engineered classroom design. In an engineered-design classroom, stimuli and consequences are manipulated in accordance with behavior modification methodology. As a part of this methodology, checkmarks were given for starting and working on tasks and appropriate classroom behavior. The checkmarks could later be redeemed for back-up reinforcers. The control condition consisted of any approach the teacher selected, including components of the engineered design except use of tangible or token rewards.

The experimental and control conditions were assigned to six different classes. Class one maintained the experimental condition for the entire project year. Class two maintained the control condition for the entire project year. Classes three and four began under the control condition but were abruptly introduced to the experimental condition at midyear. Classes five and six started as experimental and then abruptly shifted to the control at midyear.

Results.   (1) Attention to task was significantly facilitated by the experimental condition. (2) Removal of the experimental condition from classes which had become accustomed to it over a one semester period also facilitated task attention. (3) Gains in arithmetic fundamentals were significantly correlated with the presence of the experimental condition. (4) Reading achievement was not significantly affected by either the experimental or control condition.

Hillman, B.W. "The effect of knowledge of results and token reinforcement on arithmetic achievement of elementary school children." *Arithmetic Teacher* (1970), *17*, 676-82.

Purpose.   The three primary purposes of the study were to determine: (1) if per-item knowledge of results (KR) would increase arithmetic achievement more than the typical classroom situation, (2) if per-item KR plus token reinforcement would increase arithmetic achievement more than the typical classroom situation, and (3) if per-item KR plus token reinforcement would increase arithmetic achievement more than KR alone.

Subjects. There were 101 students enrolled in two regular fifth grade classes in two different schools in Parkrose School District just outside of Portland, Oregon, who served as subjects. Within each school the subjects were randomly assigned to one of three treatment subgroups. There were 34 subjects in treatment group *A*, 34 subjects in treatment group *B*, and 34 subjects in treatment group *C*.

Procedure. One male teacher was selected within each school to teach a common arithmetic unit to all the subjects in his building. All the children in each school were instructed together in a large group setting. After all of them were given instruction in arithmetic together, the subjects in each of the treatment conditions returned to three separate classrooms, where they were assigned identical twenty-problem work sheets.

After all the subjects in group *A* (the per-item KR group) had completed the first problem, the correct answer was read immediately. The same procedure was followed after they completed each problem.

Group *B* (the token reinforcement group) followed the same procedure as group *A*, except in addition the subjects were told to place a "C" mark beside the response when it was correct. A "C" mark could be redeemed for one piece of candy.

Group *C* (the control group) was given KR twenty-four hours after the assignment had been finished. They did not receive a tangible incentive for completing their work.

Results. The per-item KR group and the per-item KR plus token reinforcement group achieved higher than the control group, which had KR delayed twenty-four hours. The token reinforcement plus KR group achieved no more than the KR alone group.

Kuypers, D. S., W. C. Becker, and K. D. O'Leary. "How to make a token system fail." *Exceptional Children (1968), 35,* 101-9.

Purpose. The purpose of the study was to clarify the important components of effective token systems. An attempt was made to make clear the things that can go wrong if a token system is implemented without full consideration of the many variables important to success.

Subjects. Six third-grade and six fourth-grade children who were described as socially maladjusted served as subjects.

Procedure. Data were collected during a baseline phase, token reinforcement phase, and return to baseline or reversal phase.

Results. The average percentage of deviant behavior was significantly lower during the token reinforcement phase. However, the investigators concluded that the data on individual students and the generalization measures that were obtained indicated that the program was only marginally effective.

Comment.   An excellent discussion as to why the token program failed to be as successful as the researchers had hoped was presented. Some of the pitfalls to avoid were made clear. We highly recommend that you read this report carefully.

Madsen, C. H., W. C. Becker, and D. R. Thomas. "Rules, praise and ignoring: Elements of elementary classroom control." *Journal of Applied Behavior Analysis* (1968), *1*, 139-50.

Purpose.   The study was undertaken to ascertain the effects on classroom behavior of using rules, ignoring undesirable behaviors, and showing approval for appropriate behaviors. The study was actually a refinement of a study by Becker, Madsen, and C. R. Arnold in 1967.

Subjects.   Two children in a second grade classroom and one in a kindergarten class served as subjects. All three subjects were boys who exhibited a high frequency of problem behaviors.

Procedures.

> Previously developed behavioral categories (Becker *et al.*, 1967) were modified for use with these particular children, and baseline recordings were made to determine the frequency of problem behaviors. At the end of the baseline period the teachers entered a workshop on applications of behavioral principles to the classroom which provided them with the rationale and principles behind the procedures being introduced in their classes. Various experimental procedures were then introduced, one at a time, and the effects on the target children's behaviors observed . . . .
>   In the middle-primary class (Class A) the experimental conditions may be summarized as consisting of *Baseline*; introduction of *Rules; Rules* plus *Ignoring* deviant behavior; *Rules* plus *Ignoring* plus *Praise* for appropriate behavior; return to Baseline; and finally reinstatement of *Rules, Ignoring* and *Praise.* In the kindergarten class (Class B) the experimental conditions consisted of *Baseline*; introduction of *Rules*; Ignoring inappropriate Behavior (without continuing to emphasize rules); and the combination of *Rules, Ignoring,* and *Praise* (pp. 140-43).

Results.

> Major changes in Inappropriate Behaviors occurred only when Praise or Approval for Appropriate Behaviors was emphasized in the experimental procedures. A *t*-test, comparing average Inappropriate Behavior in conditions where Praise was not emphasized, was significant at the 0.05 level ($df = 2$) (p. 146).

Conclusions.

> The main conclusions were that: (a) Rules alone exerted little effect on classroom behavior, (b) Ignoring Inappropriate Behavior and showing approval for Appropriate Behavior (in combination) were very effective in

achieving better classroom behavior, and (c) showing approval for Appropriate Behaviors is probably the key to effective classroom management (p. 139).

McKenzie, H. S., M. Clark, M. M. Wolf, R. Kothera, and C. Benson. "Behavior modification of children with learning disabilities using grades as tokens and allowances as back-up reinforcers." *Exceptional Children* (1968), *34*, 745-52.

Purpose. The purpose of the study was to ascertain whether pay for grades could increase academic behavior to levels higher than those achieved with the usually available school incentives.

Subjects. The subjects were eight boys and two girls in a learning disabilities class which was located in a suburban elementary school in Shawnee Mission, Kansas. The subjects ranged in age from 10 to 13 years and were selected for the learning disabilities class on the basis that, although their ability levels were above the educable mentally retarded range, their achievement levels were retarded by at least two years in one or more academic areas.

Procedure. Data were collected on attending behavior throughout a baseline period and pay-for-weekly-grades period. During the baseline phase privileges available in most schools were made contingent upon the successful completion of assignments. These privileges included: recess, free time activities, eating in the school cafeteria with other children, receiving the attention of the teacher, and weekly reports to take home with high grades. All procedures employed during the baseline period were continued during the pay-for-weekly-grades period. However, the weekly grades of the baseline period were reinforced by the payment of a weekly allowance on the basis of the children's grades.

Results. An analysis of the data collected indicated that the token reinforcement system led to substantial gains in attending to reading and arithmetic for nearly all the students as compared to gains made during the baseline period.

Comment. Apparently the use of grades as tokens with allowances as back-up reinforcers can increase levels of academic behavior beyond those maintained by the application of many other incentives available to a school. However, parent cooperation would be essential to-the successful implementation of a pay-for-grades token reinforcement system.

Nolen, P. A., P. Harold, H. P. Kungelmann, and N. G. Haring. "Behavior modification in a junior high learning disabilities classroom." *Exceptional Children* (1967), *34*, 163-68.

Purpose. The purpose of the study was to determine the effects of organizing a special education classroom on a behavioral basis upon the academic response rates of adolescent students.

Subjects. The subjects were six students enrolled in a junior high school classroom. The students ranged from 12 to 16 years in age, with individual achievement levels ranging from preschool to the sixth grade.

Procedure. The academic response rates of the students were recorded during a 100-day period which included a five-day reversal or control period. In addition, data were collected from anecdotal records and achievement test scores.

During the experimental phase points were given by the teacher to the children for successful completion of each of a number of gradually lengthening academic tasks (reading and math). Points earned were redeemable at any time for play periods analogous to school recesses or free time to participate in handicrafts, typing, wood working, organized games, or science units.

Results. All subjects showed significant academic gains while the classroom was organized on a behavioral basis as compared to when it was not.

Comment. The results of this study would tend to show that the academic gains of students can be influenced by making high probability behaviors contingent upon the performance of low probability behaviors (the Premack principle).

O'Leary, K. D. and W. C. Becker. "Behavior modification of an adjustment class: A token reinforcement program." *Exceptional Children* (1967), *33*, 637-42.

Purpose. The purposes of the study were to devise a token reinforcement program which could be employed by one teacher and to see if a token system could be withdrawn gradually without an increase in disruptive behavior by transferring control to grades, praise, and teacher attention, with less frequent exchange of tokens for back-up reinforcers.

Subjects. The subjects were seventeen nine-year-old children described as emotionally disturbed with I.Q. scores (Kulhmann-Anderson) ranging from 80 to 107. The children had been assigned to an adjustment class because they displayed inappropriate classroom behaviors such as temper tantrums, crying, uncontrolled laughter, and fighting.

Procedure. Data on deviant behaviors were recorded on observation sheets during a baseline and token reinforcement phase. During the baseline period the teacher was requested to handle the children as she usually did. During the token reinforcement period the children received ratings of their behaviors and good ratings were redeemable for back-up reinforcers such as perfume, kites, and candy. With the exception of the first week, the teacher made the ratings and conducted the token system with no outside help. In order to transfer control from the token reinforcers to the more traditional methods of teacher praise and attention, the back-up reinforcers were gradually delayed over longer periods of time. In addition, the number of appropriate behaviors that would have to be exhibited to obtain a prize gradually increased.

Results. The average daily percentage of deviant behavior ranged from 66 to 91 during the baseline period and 3 to 32 during the token program. The average for all children during the token reinforcement period was 10 percent as compared to 76 percent during the baseline period. These results were found to be highly significant at the .001 level of probability.

Comment. The results of this study tended to demonstrate that a token program can be successfully implemented by one teacher. It should be remembered, however, that help was provided the teacher during the first week. According to the authors a token program can be gradually withdrawn in favor of grades, praise, and teacher attention without an accompanying large observable increase in disruptive behavior.

Phillips, E. L. "Achievement place: Token reinforcement procedures in a homestyle rehabilitation setting for 'pre-delinquent' boys." *Journal of Applied Behavior* (1968), *1*, 213-23.

Purpose. The purpose of the study was to determine the effects of a token economy on aggressive statements, poor grammar, tidiness, punctuality, and amount of homework completed of pre-delinquent boys.

Subjects and setting. Three boys who ranged in chronological age from 12 to 14 and in I.Q. from 85 to 120 served as subjects. All three boys were termed "pre-delinquent" since they had histories of exhibiting minor offenses such as "thefts," "fighting," and "general disruptive behavior." The three boys lived with two house-parents in a home situation in the community. The study was conducted in this community-based, home style rehabilitation setting.

Procedure. Recording of target behaviors (aggressive statements, poor grammar, tidiness, punctuality, and amount of homework completed) were taken during non-token reinforcement periods and token reinforcement periods.

During the token reinforcement periods the boys earned points for specified appropriate behavior and lost points for specified inappropriate behavior. Points were tallied on 3 by 5 in. index cards that the boys always carried with them. Thus, the points could be earned or lost immediately and points later redeemed for the back-up reinforcers (p. 214).

Results. "The frequencies of aggressive statements and poor grammar decreased while tidiness, punctuality, and amount of homework completed increased" (p. 213).

Conclusion. "It was concluded that a token reinforcement procedure, entirely dependent upon back-up reinforcers available in a home-style treatment setting, could contribute to an effective and economical rehabilitation program for pre-delinquents" (p. 213).

Sulzbacker, S. I. and J. E. Houser. "A tactic to eliminate disruptive behaviors in the classroom: Group contingent consequences." *American Journal of Mental Deficiency* (1968), *73*, 88-90.

Purpose. The purpose of this study was to determine the effects of a behavior modification technique on disruptive behaviors in a classroom for educable mentally retarded (EMR) children. The modification technique was designed so that a single teacher could collect all the relevant data and apply the procedures. The disruptive behaviors of concern were the display of the "naughty finger" (middle finger raised in an otherwise closed fist) and the subsequent verbal references and tattling regarding its occurrence.

Subjects. Fourteen EMR children served as subjects. They ranged in age from 6 to 10 years. Seven of the subjects were boys.

Procedures. Baseline data were gathered for nine days on the frequency of the disruptive behaviors (naughty finger, verbal responses, tattling). The children were then told:

> From now on there will be a special ten minute recess at the end of the day. However, if I see the naughty finger or hear about it, I will flip down one of these cards, and you will have one minute less of recess whenever this happens. Remember, every time I flip down one of these cards, all of you lose a minute from your recess (p. 88).

Data were collected for the next eighteen days while these instructions were in effect. The intervention procedure was then discontinued. Data collection was continued during this nine-day return to baseline period.

Results. The disruptive behaviors decreased significantly when the modification procedures were implemented. There was a gradual rise in the frequency of the disruptive behaviors when the modification procedures were discontinued.

Comment.

> The present tactic of applying a decelerating consequence to a group of children contingent upon the deviant behavior of an individual within that group is a convenient tactic in that it requires no extra equipment, minimal alteration of classroom routine, and very little investment of

teacher time; yet it was demonstrated to strongly affect classroom behavior (p. 90).

Wadsworth, H. G. "A motivational approach toward the remediation of learning disabled boys." *Exceptional Children* (1971), *38*, 33-41.

Purpose. This study was undertaken primarily to determine the influence of behavior modification techniques on behavior and reading of "learning disabled" students who had been designated by their teacher as having reading and behavior problems.

Subjects. Ten boys (C.A., 8 to 9) of middle-class, suburban background served as subjects.

Procedure. The boys served as their own controls. Reading performance and school behavior were dependent variables throughout the study with one exception: during Stage II school behavior was not a dependent variable. The project was divided into four stages as follows:

Stage I. The boys remained in the regular classroom. The only intervention during this two-month period was the learning disability (LD) teacher's consultation with the regular class teacher.

Stage II. During this three-month period the boys received forty-five minute tutoring sessions three times per week from a reading clinic.

Stage III. The boys were placed in a self-contained learning disability classroom for three months. A point reinforcement system was introduced.

Stage IV. During the five months of this period the boys were gradually reintegrated into the regular class setting. When they were in the regular class setting they were not reinforced with points; however, they did receive points for appropriate behavior when in the LD self-contained classroom. By the end of this period all the boys had been completely reintegrated into the regular class setting.

Results.

The rate of learning (Libaw, Berres and Coleman, 1966), based on past learning speed, was used to measure the boys against themselves. Improvement in reading level was not statistically significant ($p < .05$) during Stages I and II. Significant differences were found for Stages III and IV. In the 3 month span of Stage III, the group gained 8 months in reading performance. During the 5 month period of Stage IV, a gain of 9 months in reading level was made. . . .

It was expected that with no intervention, behavior would do no better than remain the same (and probably worsen). There were statistically significant differences in the direction of improvement during Stages I and III. . . Behavior was not considered a problem at the end of Stage III. Thus, no further improvement was expected or achieved in Stage IV (pp. 38-39).

Comment.

It can be argued that variables other than the primary one discussed (reinforcement techniques) accounted for the significant improvements in the boys' reading level and social behavior. The improvement could have been attributed to the small classroom setting, the teacher's personality, the newly found enjoyment of school, or parental support via the home...It is likely, that the positive changes were due to several variables; however, most of the credit is given to the motivational approach (p. 41).

Books and
Descriptive Reports

Abidin, R. R. "What's wrong with behavior modification." *Journal of School Psychology* (1971), *9*, 38-42.

A few of the issues, parameters, and problems which must be considered by the school psychologist and teacher before and during the implementation of behavior modification techniques into the classroom are discussed. "As a practical guide it considers preconditions to setting up a behavior modification program as well as some of the most common process errors in the use of behavior modification" [p. 38]. Preconditions discussed that should be considered before using behavior modification techniques in the classroom are: (1) an evaluation of the teacher's personality and teaching style as they relate to the operation of a behavior modification program, (2) the training the teacher must receive, and (3) the decision that must be made concerning by whom and for what the teacher will reinforce. Common process errors discussed are: (1) not correctly defining the problem behavior, (2) failing to record baseline data, (3) utilizing inappropriate reinforcers, and (4) failing of the school psychologist and teacher to recognize that behavior modification is only a tool to support good teaching. We strongly recommend that the teacher contemplating the establishment of a behavior modification program read and study this article carefully.

Axelrod, S. "Token reinforcement programs in special classes." *Exceptional Children* (1971), *37*, 371-78.

Token reinforcement programs that have been implemented in special education classrooms are reviewed. Some of the advantages of token systems are discussed in the introduction. Research studies regarding the effects of token systems on various types of behavior and with many different kinds of exceptional children are then summarized. Implications of the studies reviewed for future research are also discussed.

We strongly recommend that you read this article also.

Ayllon, T. and N. Azrin. *The token economy.* New York: Appleton-Century-Crofts, 1968.

Token reinforcement in a mental hospital setting is discussed. Topics covered include:

1. Defining the target behavior,
2. Selecting and maximizing the effectiveness of reinforcers.
3. The response-reinforcement relation,
4. The shaping of a response,
5. Evaluation of reinforcement techniques, and
6. Therapeutic and administrative considerations.

Although the setting for the development of much of the information presented was a mental hospital, many of the same procedures discussed could be applied in public school classrooms.

Becker, W. C., S. Engelmann, and D. R. Thomas. *Teaching: A course in applied psychology,* Palo Alto, Calif.: Science Research Associates, 1971.

The book is divided into two parts. Science Research Associates (1971) describes each part as follows:

> Part I. This section focuses on the use of behavior consequences to both reduce classroom problems of management or motivation and to strengthen desired classroom behavior. Essentially a behavior modification primer for the teacher, it reinforces the fact that behavior modification is an effective method for accomplishing classroom goals and not merely a set of simple tricks.
> Part II. This portion analyzes teacher sequence structuring for presenting concepts and operations which are usable outside the classroom. A general model of instruction is built to provide a basis for indicating key elements, in any teaching act. Implications of this model of teaching are examined for programming curriculum, special education problems, and stimulating the intelligent mind. What results is a specialized but comprehensive coverage of teaching as a "make learn" experience (p. 22).

Birnbrauer, J. S., S. W. Bijou, M. M. Wolf, and J. D. Kidder. "Programmed instruction in the classroom." In L. P. Ullman and L. Krasner (eds.), *Case studies in behavior modification.* New York: Holt, Rinehart, & Winston, Inc., 1965, 358-63.

A project that involved eight intermediate age educable mentally retarded (EMR) children for one academic year is described. The project had two major purposes: (1) to develop programmed instructional materials in academic subjects for EMR studies and (2) to develop procedures based on reinforcement principles to motivate cooperation, concentration, perseverance, and good study habits.

The programmed instructional materials were designed to be self-instructional. In order to give these materials a chance to be successful, a special classroom with a routine that would permit children to follow independent, staggered schedules was designed. After it was discovered that the students would not work steadily for only social approval and knowledge of results, a token reinforcement system was implemented. Stars, along with verbal approval, were dispensed when a student exhibited appropriate behavior or answered questions correctly. Later, stars were replaced by checkmarks. The stars (or checkmarks) could be redeemed for back-up reinforcers such as airplane models. An example of one child's progress is included to show the benefits of the program.

Buckley, N. K. and H. M. Walker. *Modifying classroom behavior: A manual of procedures for classroom teachers.* Champaign, Ill.: Research Press, 1970.

This manual was written specifically for classroom teachers and prospective teachers. The format of the book presents the content in a semi-programmed fashion; that is, some of the material is programmed and some of it is not. The book is divided into two parts — basic principles and application. Under part I the authors discuss the following topics:

1. How behaviors are learned through reinforcement, modeling and shaping,
2. The reasons behaviors are maintained,
3. The elimination of behaviors through punishment, extinction, time-out, counterconditioning, stimulus satiation, and stimulus change, and
4. How and what behaviors should be measured. Part II provides ample illustrations of practical applications of the principles discussed in Part I.

Christoplos, F. C. and P. Valletutti. "Defining behavior modification." *Educational Technology* (1969), *9*, 28-30.

Since changing behavior *per se* has always been the goal of educational programs, the authors focus their attention on what is new and different about behavior modification. They state that the main innovation in behavior modification is its emphasis on evaluation or measurement techniques; that is, techniques of determining how effectively behavior is modified in the direction desired by the teacher. Three aspects in the evaluation and measurement of the effectiveness of behavior modification are briefly discussed. These three aspects are: (1) evaluation or diagnosis of the child, (2) analysis and sequencing of task, and (3) procedural methods and management techniques.

Curry, D. R. "Case studies in behavior modification." *Psychology in the Schools* (1970), *7*, 330-35.

Two case studies in which behavior modification techniques were utilized to alleviate classroom problem behaviors are presented.

The first case dealt with an eight-year-old second grade girl's lack of progress in learning to read, despite the fact she possessed above average intelligence and had no demonstrated physical disabilities. The girl's reading improved by making parent and teacher attention and time to read (although she was a poor reader, she liked to read) contingent upon "good reading."

The second case involved a six-year-old boy enrolled in the first grade who exhibited aggressive and disruptive behavior in the classroom. Being able to engage in each recess period (there were five each day) was made contingent on not physically attacking any other student or verbally disrupting the class during the time immediately preceding the recess period. The child's aggressive and disruptive behaviors decreased considerably after this intervention technique was implemented.

Deibert, A. N. and A. J. Harmon. *New tool for changing behavior.* Champaign, Ill.: Research Press, 1970.

The book was written for parents, physicians, and teachers who might be interested in a brief and nontechnical discussion of behavior modification. The book is divided into two parts. In the first part the authors discuss the basic principles and techniques of behavior modification. Many examples of how these principles and techniques can be applied in everyday life are included. Part II provides illustrations of clinical applications of behavioral laws. The questions some people often raise about behavior modification being a cold and mechanical approach are answered throughout the book.

Edlund, C. V. "Rewards at home to promote desirable school behavior." *Teaching Exceptional Children* (1969), *1*, 121-27.

A program in which reinforcers, available in most home environments, were used to enhance appropriate classroom behavior is described. Appropriate school behavior was defined as a child "(a) increasing the number of accurately completed class assignments within the time allotted for the completion of the task in question, and (b) increasing the length of time during which his social and personal behavior meets classroom standards" (p. 122).

How the program was organized through parent-teacher conferences is discussed. A checklist was devised whereby the teacher could record whether or not a child had displayed the designated appropriate behavior during school hours. Parents were instructed in how to make their child's amount of free time to play and watch television contingent upon the amount of appropriate behavior he exhibited in school as indicated to them by a checklist sent home by the child's teacher. A discussion of how the reward system was gradually phased out after the children learned appropriate school behaviors is included. How to handle such problems as the child failing to bring home the checklist or the child forging recordings on the checklist is also discussed.

Exceptional Children (1970), *37*, 83-176.

This publication illustrates the growing interest of educators in the principles and techniques of behavior modification. This entire issue of the journal was devoted to this topic. The first article, by Thomas Lovitt, discusses the general concerns of behavior modifiers. Present-day behavior modification programs are put into historical perspective by Steven Forness and Donald MacMillan in the second article. Also included in this journal are articles which report on:

1. Language training for the severely language handicapped,
2. The management of out-of-seat behavior by a timer-game,
3. The use of behavior modification with head start children,
4. Precision techniques that can be used to manage teacher and child behaviors,
5. The training of consulting teachers to assist elementary teachers in the management and education of exceptional children, and
6. The effects of loud and soft reprimands on disruptive behaviors of students.

Lovitt closes out the journal by pointing out what he considers to be some of the future trends in behavior modification. While we recommend that you read the entire journal, it is almost imperative that you read both articles by Lovitt and the one by Forness and MacMillan.

Fargo, G. A., C. Behrns, and P. Nolen. *Behavior modification in the classroom.* Belmont, Calif.: Wadsworth Publishing Co., Inc., 1970.

In the preface to this book the authors provide a brief statement of purpose and a description of the material included in the text.

This text is designed primarily for teachers and students in teacher training who seek practical answers to classroom management. The articles have been selected and abridged to present available research findings in a nontechnical and easily applicable format. The book is divided into sections and subsections based on theoretical issues, age groups, disability types, and interdisciplinary participation, but the editors emphasize in their introductions the generalization of techniques across these categorical headings. The articles included are not all from the classroom arena, but the techniques illustrated do lend themselves to classroom application.

In Section 1, the text explores the pros and cons of the current ethical and theoretical debate over behavior modification as used in the educational management of children. The second section, subdivided by age group, contains articles that illustrate the management of motor skills, language development, cognitive skills, and the modification of undesirable behavior. Although the editors recognize the artificial nature of the labels applied to disability groupings of children, we suggest that labeling of specific educational tasks is useful. In the third section, techniques are applied across the artificial label designations currently in use. Effective educational management requires the cooperation of the classroom teacher with all persons in contact with the child, including social workers, administrators, psychologists, psychiatrists, counselors, speech therapists, and parents. The final section samples articles that reflect the potential of this interdependence (pp. ix-x).

Forness, S. R. "Behavioristic approach to classroom management and motivation." *Psychology in the Schools* (1970), *7*, 356-62.

A review of some of the basis principles of behavior modification that can be applied in the classroom is presented. Topics discussed include a definition of reinforcement, primary and secondary reinforcement, the use of teacher attention, the use of ignoring and time-out techniques, observation and measurement of observable behavior, the Premack principle, respondent conditioning approaches, and limitations of behavior modification. We strongly suggest that the novice in behavior modification read and study this article before implementing any type of formal behavioristic approach in the classroom.

Girardeau, F. L. and J. E. Spradin. "Token rewards in a cottage program." *Mental Retardation* (1964), *2*, 345-51.

Behavioral principles were applied to specific behaviors of trainable adolescence girls. The focus of the reinforcement stressed improvement of behavior rather than task completion. Such aspects as the store, the cost, and behavior changes that occurred were also discussed.

Green, R. L. and T. J. Stachnik. "Money, motivation, and academic achievement." *Phi Delta Kappan* (1968), *50*, 228-30.

A method to motivate disadvantaged children to achieve academically is discussed. It is suggested that money, as an external reinforcer, could be used to motivate these children so that they will *want to learn*. Some criticisms of such an approach that might occur are set forth and answered. In addition, the cost of such a monetary reward system is discussed.

Grieger, R. N., J. B. Mordock, and N. Breyer. "General guidelines for conducting behavior modification programs in public school settings." *Journal of School Psychology* (1970), *8*, 259-66.

The abstract to this article adequately describes its contents.

> Tentative guidelines for initiating behavior modification programs are presented. Discussion focuses on the importance of initial introduction of these procedures to teachers, the relation of teacher personality variables to technique selection, factors to consider when evaluating children for modification, and suggestions for on-going participation and withdrawal of the psychologist as an active agent in such programs (p. 259).

Homme, L., A. P. Csanyi, M. A. Gonzales, and J. R. Rechs. *How to use contingency contracting in the classroom.* Champaign, Ill.: Research Press, 1969.

One approach to the systematic use of reinforcement principles to motivate children is presented. The approach is labeled *contingency contracting*, and it teaches a basic rule of behavior in a clear and understandable way, the basic rule being that whether a behavior is strengthened or weakened depends upon its consequences. Contingency contracting, as discussed by Homme and his associates, makes use of a principle set forth by David Premack (1959, 1965). This principle simply states that an activity that a person generally likes to engage in can be used as a reinforcer for an activity the person generally does not like to do. The principle is in operation when a child is told that when he finishes a specified number of arithmetic problems correctly he can go to the gymnasium and play basketball for ten minutes.

The book is divided into two parts. The first part provides information about how contingency contracting works. In the second part, applications that can be made of contingency contracting in the classroom setting are outlined.

Journal of Applied Behavior Analysis, published by the Society for the Experimental Analysis of Behavior. (Readers wishing to subscribe to this journal can write: Mary Louise Sherman, Business Manager, Dept. of Human Development, University of Kansas, Lawrence, Kansas, 66044).

Each journal is devoted primarily to publication of reports regarding the analysis of behavior. A few technical articles pertinent to behavioral research and discussions of issues concerning the application of behavioral principles can also be found in this journal. At least elementary understanding of behavior modification methodology, research design, and statistics is needed to understand the majority of the reports presented in the journal.

Kauffman, J. M. "Recent trends in the behavioral approach to educating disturbed children." *Journal of School Health* (1970), *40*, 271-72.

Recent trends in behavior modification are discussed. Position papers and research which tend to support the trends postulated are included. Also presented are some of the limitations of behavior modification that are beginning to be recognized. This article is excellent for readers interested in getting some idea as to the trends in behavior modification.

Kazdin, A. E. "Toward a client administered token reinforcement program." *Education and training of the mentally retarded* (1971), *6*, 52-55.

How clients (C.A., 16 to 52; I.Q., untestable to 85) in a sheltered workshop were utilized in a token reinforcement program to dispense reinforcers to other clients is discussed. Case materials on several clients who were involved are presented. In the concluding remarks, the advantages of having the clients dispense the reinforcers over the usual practice wherein only the staff members are allowed to handle the reinforcers are outlined.

Keller, F. S. *Learning: Reinforcement theory.* New York: Random House, Inc., 1968.

Several statements made by Professor E. L. Hartley in the preface to the book adequately describe its contents.

> In this paper, Professor Fred S. Keller provides a simple and brief introduction to the reinforcement theory of learning. Simple and brief though it is, all of the fundamental principles are identified, clarified, and their interrelationships and possible extensions indicated. It is, therefore, more than just the exposition of a theory of learning: it provides a learning-theory approach to all of Psychology. Though written simply, there has been no sacrifice of accuracy and scientific caution. This, then, is a document that will be appreciated not only by beginning students, but also by professionals who have found the customary expositions too technical or too bulky (p. v).

If you haven't done so, be sure to read this very excellent but short book (37 pages) to gain a better understanding of the fundamental principles of reinforcement theory.

MacMillan, D. L. and S. R. Forness. "Behavior modification: Limitations and liabilities." *Exceptional Children* (1970), *37*, 291-97.

MacMillan and Forness discuss what they consider to be the major limitations of behavior modification. These limitations include: the oversimplification of the human situation by the behavioristic paradigm; the failure of behavior modification theory to guide teachers in establishing appropriate goals; a view of motivation as completely extrinsic in nature; heavy reliance on arbitrary as opposed to natural reinforcers; a limited definition of reinforcement (a stimulus which increases the probability of a response) that ignores certain cognitive aspects of reinforcement; and the tremendous potential for misuse. After discussing each of the above possible limitations, the authors drew several conclusions that they feel should be heeded by the rigid behaviorist.

Madsen, C. H. and C. K. Madsen. *Teaching/Discipline: Behavioral principles toward a positive approach.* Boston: Allyn & Bacon, Inc., 1970.

Written specifically for teachers and prospective teachers, this book can be used as an excellent guide when using behavioral principles to aid in classroom discipline. Discussions concerning practical applications of behavioral principles in the classroom are presented. Questions answered include:

1. What constitutes a reward?
2. Can contingencies be structured?
3. Is consistency difficult?
4. Can behavior be measured?

We highly recommend that you read this book carefully before implementing any specific type of reinforcement system.

Madsen, C. K. "How reinforcement techniques work." *Music Educators Journal* (1971), *57*, 38-41.

Several studies concerning behavior modification as it relates to music are discussed. The studies discussed fall into two general classifications. One group of studies explored the use of music to reinforce nonmusical behaviors. The other group was concerned with the use of behavioral principles to reinforce specific music experiences. This article would be excellent for the person interested in how reinforcement principles can be used in the teaching of music, as well as how music can be used as a reinforcing event.

Martin, G. L. and R. B. Powers. "Attention span: An operant conditioning analysis." *Exceptional Children* (1967), *33*, 565-69.

The authors suggest in the introduction that a major result of the current usage of the concept of short attention span has been to hinder the education of brain damaged and retarded students. In other words, this concept has been used by some educators as an excuse for not attempting to provide the retarded child with educational experiences he might otherwise receive. After discussing the current usage of the concept, an operant conditioning analysis of attention span is presented. The authors cite research to support their contention that, within an operant conditioning framework, a short attention span should not be viewed as an unmanipulable entity. They suggest that teachers can use an operant conditioning approach to improve attending behavior in brain damaged and retarded students.

O'Hara, E. A. "Using pay to change mentally retarded students' work behavior." *Teaching Exceptional Children* (1970), *2*, 163-69.

An in-class work-study program conducted at the Del Campo High School, Fair Oaks, California, for mentally retarded high school freshmen, sophomores, and juniors is described. The work-study program consisted of paid and unpaid work sessions in a simulated top repair shop. "The program had two objectives: (a) to test the effectiveness of using operant techniques to teach work and social skills considered important to successful performance, and (b) to determine the effectiveness of using money payments as incentives for achieving the skills in question" (p. 163). How work and social behaviors were rewarded and changes that occurred in student behavior as a result are discussed.

Patterson, G. R. and M. E. Gullion. *Living with children: New methods for parents and teachers.* Champaign, Ill.: Research Press, 1968.

This book is written in down-to-earth language and in programmed form to make it easy reading for the novice in behavior modification. The book is divided into two sections. The first section is about how parents and children learn. Such questions as what reinforcers are, how reinforcers can be used to change children's behaviors, and how children's behaviors can be observed are included in this section. Families and children with extreme problem behaviors are described in the six chapters that comprise Section II.

> Each of the chapters represents a different family; each chapter also outlines the "treatment program" that was used in the case. The general approach was to teach the parents the principles of social learning, and then to work in the home demonstrating how these principles could be used to help that child and that family. In all cases, the parents were trained to "do" their own treatment; and most of these parents were successful in making major changes in the behavior of their children (p. 64).

Sattler, H. E. and K. S. Swoope. "Token systems: A procedural guide." *Psychology in the Schools* (1970), *7*, 363-84.

Procedural guidelines for establishing a token economy are presented. The following ten topics are briefly discussed: the selection of desirable behaviors, the selection of the tokens to be dispensed, the selection of the back-up reinforcers, procedures for informing the pupils which behaviors will be rewarded, methods for dispensing tokens, the recording of procedures for keeping an accurate record of the number of tokens dispensed, the process of exchanging tokens for back-up reinforcers, the establishment of ways of making back-up reinforcers available, a method for bringing the reinforcing activity period to an end, and the selection of the type of contingency (group or individual) to be used when awarding tokens. This article should be read before implementing token systems.

Sloggett, B. B. "Use of group activities and team rewards to increase individual classroom productivity." *Teaching Exceptional Children* (1971), *3*, 54-65.

"This article describes how a token reinforcement system was used to reward group rather than individual behavior in order to promote academic development among low-achieving adolescent Hawaiian boys" [p. 54]. The boys were enrolled in a self-contained special class in an intermediate school. They were described as demonstrating social and academic problem behaviors that interfered with their school achievement. Why and how these problem behaviors were brought under control by the reinforcement of group rather than individual behaviors is discussed. An explanation is given as to why Hawaiians might respond better to group reinforcement procedures. "Hawaiians apparently derive little personal pleasure from competing successfully against others and, in fact, avoid individual competition." According to Gallimore and Howard (1968), "Hawaiians are motivated primarily by peer pressure, affiliation, and avoidance of social disapproval" [p. 55]. Taking this fact into consideration, the students were divided into teams and group goals were established. Peer approval was received by each child when he displayed appropriate behavior since the team received a reward as a result.

Ullman, L. P. and L. Krasner. *Case studies in behavior modification.* New York: Holt, Rinehart & Winston, Inc., 1966.

Case studies that illustrate what can be done to mitigate and change maladaptive behavior are presented. The apparent purpose is not to validate behavior modification, but rather to provide examples of what is being done with behavior modification procedures. Many of the illustrations included involve disturbed or retarded persons who were functioning in a mental hospital or other special setting.

Valett, R. E. "A social reinforcement technique for the classroom management of behavior disorders." *Exceptional Children* (1966), *33*, 185-89.

A model social reinforcement technique applicable to regular and special class students is discussed. The technique presented integrates both secondary and primary reinforcers. It is based on a continuous evaluation of pupil behavior and careful and systematic programming of educational experiences. Under this model a weekly work and reward record is kept by each student to give him a clear and highly visible picture of his progress and accomplishments at all times.

Whelan, R. E. and N. Haring. "Modification and maintenance of behavior through systematic application of consequences." *Exceptional Children* (1966), *32*, 281-89.

How some of the basic principles of behavior modification can be applied in the classroom to change children's observable behaviors is discussed. Research and illustrations which tend to demonstrate the effectiveness of precise and systematic application of behavioral principles are included. The authors first build a rationale to support their contention that educators should apply behavioral principles in the classroom to decrease inappropriate and accelerate and maintain appropriate behavior. They then discuss the importance of applying behavior modification principles and techniques with precision. The dangers of applying these techniques in a random and haphazard fashion are included. This article should be read before attempting to implement a formal, planned program of behavioral modification.

Films*

Behavior theory in practice: Experiments in operant behavior. 16 mm, 21 min., color, Indiana University, rental fee $7.50.

Behavior theory in practice: Generalization, discrimination. 16 mm, 22 min., color, Indiana University, rental fee $7.50.

Behavior theory in practice: Sequence of behavior. 16 mm, 19 min., color, Indiana University, rental fee $7.50.

Behavior theory in practice: Shaping various operants, various species. 16 mm, 21 min., color, Indiana University, rental fee $7.50.

---

*The authors would like to express their appreciation to Dr. James M. Kauffman for his assistance with reviewing films pertaining to behavior modification.

These four films are a series that demonstrate the various behaviorism concepts, primarily with animals. They present a clear and precise representation of these concepts.

Rewards and reinforcement. 16 mm, 26 min., b & w, Indiana University, rental fee $7.25.

In this film a plan is set forth in which the teacher decides what he wants the child to do and what the child will work for, breaks the task down into small steps, and reinforces the child for approximations. Examples with disadvantaged, retarded, speech handicapped, and normal children are included.

Reinforcement in learning and extinction. 16 mm, 8 min., b & w, Indiana University, rental fee $3.15.

This film presents pigeons in a laboratory setting to show how basic principles of learning take place. It shows application of principles to human beings.

Achievement place. 16mm, 25 min., b & w, University of Kansas, rental fee $5.00.

This film demonstrates the application of a token economy to the behavior of pre-delinquent boys in a home-style residential setting.

Controlling behavior through reinforcement. 16 mm, 18 min., b & w, Indiana University, rental fee $5.50.

Principles are demonstrated in a laboratory setting with animals with extension to the classroom setting.

Learning. 16 mm, 26 min., color, CRM publications (produced by *Psychology Today*), rental fee $35.00.

This film shows basic behavior principles in laboratory and natural settings. It also includes interviews with Skinner, Azrin, and Malott.

Behavioral modification: Teaching language to psychiatric children. 16 mm, 40 min., color, Appleton-Century-Crofts, rental fee $30.00.

This film shows details of language development in autistic children at the Neuro-psychiatric Institute (NPI), UCLA. It includes interviews with Lovaas and Simmon and excellent examples of behavior shaping, stimulus control, and punishment.

Behavior therapy. 16 mm, 40 min., b & w, Southeastern Instructional Materials Center (SEIMC), George Washington University, no rental fee.

This film shows behavior modification being used with autistic children, schizophrenic adults, and severely retarded children. Interviews are conducted with Birnbrauer and Lovaas.

Behavior therapy with an autistic child. 16 mm, 30 min., b & w, National Institute of Health, no rental fee.

This unedited film shows the assessment of an autistic child using behavior modification techniques.

Learning and behavior. 16 mm, 25 min., b & w, Pennsylvania State University, rental fee $8.00.

Behavioral principles are demonstrated with animals in a laboratory. Charles Collingsworth interviews Skinner and Hernstein.

The Santa Monica Project. 16 mm, 20 min., color, SEIMC, George Washington University, no rental fee.

This film shows the engineered classroom developed by Hewett. It includes classroom design, curriculum, and reinforcement systems.

Autism's lonely children. 16 mm, 20 min., b & w, Indiana University, rental fee $4.60.

This film shows Hewett at NPI, UCLA working with autistic children.

Future
Research Needs

Before 1960 there were few applied classroom research projects reported on the effects of systematically implementing behavior modification programs designed to change children's behavior. During the 1960s and early 1970s we have witnessed a tremendous increase in the number of research studies on the effects of behavior modification on children's behavior within the classroom setting. There is, however (partly because of the success of past research) much more to be done. Some future research needs include:

1. More research such as that done by O'Leary and Becker (1967) on the feasibility of having one teacher alone apply a planned behavior modification program should be conducted. Most of the research to date has evaluated the effectiveness of behavior modification techniques in a classroom where at least one teacher and several aides in the form of university students and/or the researcher himself were involved.

2. There is a need for adequately designed longitudinal research to find out what happens in adult life to children who are exposed to a planned behavior modification approach as opposed to children who are not.

3. The results of additional research on effective ways of teaching reinforcement principles to teachers, parents, and aides who would help improve training programs in behavior modification. Becker *et al.* (1967) explored a kind of direct written rules to follow method of helping teachers apply reinforcement principles and found it effective. Hawkins *et al.* (1966) found hand signals and lights to be effective in helping parents learn to discriminate when to reinforce and when to ignore. Andrews (1970) trained elementary teachers in a four-week inservice pilot program to apply behavior modification principles. The teachers were able to modify the children's behaviors in their classrooms effectively as a result of their participation in the training sessions.

4. More research such as that done by Gardner, Brust, and Watson (1970), concerning the development of scales to measure a teacher's skills in applying behavior modification techniques, would be of value. Valid and reliable tests to measure knowledge in behavior modification and instruments to evaluate a person's skill in applying that knowledge would improve training programs in behavior modification greatly. The professor and prospective teacher would have feedback as to the effectiveness of the training program.

5. More investigations regarding the use of the Premack principle in the classroom should be conducted. This evidence may lead to greater use of rewards already available in the classroom.

6. Work in the area of training pupils to manage the dispensation of the tokens themselves, such as that by Kazdin (1971) with clients in a sheltered workshop, is needed. If children could be taught to administer the token program themselves the teacher would be relieved of a great deal of work in the day-to-day operation of the system.

7. Research is needed on what effect rewarding specific behaviors has on the total classroom environment. Chapter 8 of this book describes a study that evaluated changes in certain behaviors that occurred as a result of reinforcing other behaviors.

8. More studies concerned with *when* it is feasible to shift from a continuous to an intermittent reinforcement schedule are needed.

9. Work is needed regarding the best way to gradually transfer children from a token reinforcement system to a social reinforcement system.

10. Studies are needed regarding ways to make it easier to establish token systems; we know they work, but what is the easiest and most efficient way to implement and operate such a system in the classroom.

Presently an extraordinary amount of time and effort is required for a teacher to establish and operate a token system by himself successfully.

11. Few people would argue about the efficacy of behavior modification; however, ways to help increase generalization (the behavior changed in one particular setting or time applied to other settings or times) needs to be investigated.

References

Andrews, J. K., "The results of a pilot program to train teachers in the classroom application of behavior modifications techniques." *Journal of School Psychology* (1970), *8*, 37-42.

Becker, W. C., C. H. Madsen, C. R. Arnold, and D. R. Thomas, "The contingent use of teacher attention and praise in reducing classroom behavior problems." *The Journal of Special Education* (1967), *1*, 287-307.

Gallimore, R. and A. Howard, "Studies in a Hawaiian community: Na Makamaka o Nanakuli." *Pacific Anthropological Record,* Bishop Museum, Department of Anthropology (1968), 1.

Gardner, J. M., D. J. Brust, and L. S. Watson, "A scale to measure skill in applying modification techniques to the mentally retarded." *American Journal of Mental Deficiency* (1970), *74*, 633-36.

Hawkins, R. P., R. F. Peterson, E. Schweid, and S. W. Bijou, "General guidelines for conducting behavior modification programs in public school settings." *Journal of Social Psychology* (1970), *8*, 259-66.

Kazdin, A. E., "Toward a client administered token reinforcement program." *Education and Training of the Mentally Retarded* (1971), *6*, 52-55.

Libaw, F., F. Berres, and J. Coleman. "Evaluating the treatment of learning difficulties." In N.J. Long, W. C. Morse, and R. G. Newman (eds.), *Conflict in the classroom: The education of emotionally disturbed children.* Belmont, California: Wadsworth Publishing Company, Inc., 1965, 505-8.

O'Leary, K. D. and W. C. Becker, "Behavior modification of an adjustment class: A token reinforcement program." *Exceptional Children* (1967), *33*, 637-42.

Patterson, G. R. and M. E. Gullion, *Living with children: New methods for parents and teachers.* Champaign, Illinois: Research Press, 1968.

Premack, D. "Toward empirical behavior laws: I. Positive reinforcement." *Psychological Review* (1959), *66*, 219-33.

_____"Reinforcement theory." In D. Levine (ed.), *Nebraska symposium on motivation.* Lincoln: University of Nebraska Press, 1965.

Science Research Associates, *Materials for professional educators*, 1971.

Wood, F. H., "Behavior modification techniques in context." *Newsletter of the Council for Children with Behavioral Disorders* (1968), *5*, 12-15.

Additional Materials

Abbott, M. S. "Modification of the classroom behavior of a disadvantaged kindergarten boy by social reinforcement and isolation." *Journal of Education* (1969), *151*, 31-45.

Ashem, B. "The treatment of disaster phobia by systematic desensitization." *Behavior Research and Therapy* (1963), *1*, 81-84.

Ayllon, T. and E. Haughton. "Control of the behavior of schizophrenic patients by food." *Journal of Experimental Analysis of Behavior* (1962), *5*, 343-52.

————"Modification of symptomatic verbal behavior of mental patients." *Behavior Research and Therapy* (1964), *2*, 87-97.

Bandura, A. "Behavior modification through modeling procedures." In L. Krasner and L. P. Ullmann (eds.), *Research in behavior modification.* New York: Holt, Rinehart & Winston, Inc., 1965.

Barclary, J. R. *et al.* "Effectiveness of teacher training in social learning behavior modification techniques." *Measurement and Evaluation in Guidance* (1971), *4*, 79-89.

Baumeister, A. A. and C. C. Ward. "Effects of rewards upon the reaction times of mental defectives." *American Journal of Mental Deficiency* (1967), *71*, 801-5.

Berger, S. M. "Incidental learning through vicarious reinforcement." *Psychological Reports* (1961), *9*, 477-91.

Bijou, S. W. "Experimental studies of child behavior, normal and deviant." In L. Krasner and L. P. Ullmann (eds.), *Research in behavior modification.* New York: Holt, Rinehart & Winston, Inc., 1965.

Bijou, S. W. and R. Orlando. "Rapid development of multiple-schedule performances with retarded children." *Journal of Experimental Analysis of Behavior* (1961), *3*, 7-16.

Birnbrauer, J. S. and J. Lawler. "Token reinforcement for learning. *Mental Retardation* (1964), *2*, 275-79.

Blacker, K.H. and G. C. Stone. "Adaptation of operant conditioning techniques for use with mental patients: 1. Exploratory studies." *California Mental Health* (1963), *1*, 32-33.

Bottoms, G. and K. Reynolds. "Work experience program for behavior modification." *American Vocational Journal* (1969), *44*, 24-26.

Brackbill, Y. "Extinction of the smiling response in infants as a function of reinforcement schedule." *Child Development* (1958), *29*, 115-24.

Brown, J. C. and D. G. Teague. "Behavior modification in the school: A team approach." *School Counselor* (1971), *18*, 215-16.

Brown, L. "Using behavior modification principles to teach sight vocabulary." *Teaching Exceptional Children* (1970), *2*, 120-28.

Coundiff, W. E. and M. T. Coffman. "Token changes." *School and Community* (1969), *56*, 41.

Craddick, R. A. and M. R. Stern. "Verbal conditioning: The effect of partial reinforcement upon the recall of early memories." *Journal of Abnormal Social Psychology* (1964), *68*, 353-55.

Dinoff, M., R. F. Horner, B. S. Kurpiewski, H. C. Rickard, and E. O. Timmons. "Conditioning verbal behavior of a psychiatric population in a group therapy-like situation." *Journal of Clinical Psychology* (1960), *16*, 371-72.

Duncan, A. D. "Self-application of behavior modification techniques by teenagers." *Adolescence* (1969), *4*, 541-56.

Durio, H. F. "Reinforcement: Candy, grades, or money?" *The Texas Outlook* (1966), *50*, 17.

Ehrle, R. A. "Alternative to words in the behavior modification of disadvantaged youth." *The Vocational Guidance Quarterly* (1968), *17*, 41-46.

Ellis, N. R. "Amount of reward and operant behavior in mental defectives." *American Journal of Mental Deficiency* (1962), *66*, 595-99.

Ellis, N. R., C. D. Barnett, and M. W. Pryer. "Operant behavior in mental defectives: Exploratory studies." *Journal of Experimental Analysis of Behavior* (1960), *3*, 63-69.

Ellis, N. R. and M. W. Pryer. "Primary versus secondary reinforcement in simple discrimination learning of mental defectives." *Psychology Reports* (1958), *4*, 67-70.

Englen, R. *et al.* "Behavior modification techniques applied to a family unit: A case study." *Journal of Child Psychology* (1968), *9*, 245-52.

Fine, M. J. "Some qualifying notes on the development and implementation of behavior modification programs." *Journal of School Psychology* (1970), *8*, 301-5.

Flanagan, B., J. Goldiamond, and N. H. Azrin. "Instatement of stuttering in normally fluent individuals through operant procedures." *Science* (1959), *130*, 979-81.

Gardner, J. M. "Behavior modification research in mental retardation: Search for an adequate paradigm; operant conditioning." *American Journal of Mental Deficiency* (1969), *73*, 844-51.

Geppert, T. V. "Management of nocturnal enuresis by conditioned response." *Journal of the American Medical Association* (1953), *152*, 381-83.

George, R. L. and K. A. George. "Behavioral modification in the teaching of typewriting." *Business Education Forum* (1971), *25*, 42-43.

Giles, D. K. and M. M. Wolf. "Toilet training institutionalized severe retardates: An application of operant behavior modification techniques." *American Journal of Mental Deficiency* (1966), *70*, 766-80.

Goodlet, G. R. *et al.* "Modification of disruptive behavior of two young children and follow up one year later." *Journal of School Psychology* (1970), *8*, 60-63.

Grossberg, J. M. "Behavior therapy: A review." *Psychological Bulletin* (1964), *62*, 73-88.

Heitzman, A. J. "Effects of a token reinforcement system on the reading and arithmetic skills learnings of migrant primary school pupils." *The Journal of Educational Research* (1970), *63*, 455-58.

Henchy, V. "Use of token reinforcement as a means of improving the self-help skills of a group of trainable retarded children." *Graduate Research in Education and Related Disciplines* (1971), *5*, 124-36.

Himelstein, P. "Use of behavior modification procedures in MR classes." *The Journal for Special Educators of the Mentally Retarded* (1969), *6*, 68-71.

Holz, W. C., N. H. Azrin, and T. Ayllon, "Elimination of behavior of mental patients by response-produced extinction." *Journal of Experimental Analysis of Behavior* (1963), *6*, 407-12.

Homme, L. E., O. C. Debaca, J. V. Devine, R. Steinhorst, and E. J. Rickert. "Use of the Premack principle in controlling the behavior of nursery school children." *Journal of Experimental Analysis of Behavior* (1963), *6*, 544.

Jackson, M. E. and N. P. Jackson. "Educational application of behavior modification techniques with severely retarded children in a child development center; Santa Barbara, Calif." *California Journal of Educational Research* (1970), *21*, 68-73.

Jones, B. A. and R. J. Karraker. "Elementary counselor and behavior modification." *Elementary School Guidance and Counseling* (1969), *4*, 28-34.

Kanfer, F. H. and A. R. Marston. "Human reinforcement: Vicarious and direct." *Journal of Experimental Psychology* (1963), *65*, 292-96.

Krasner, L. "Behavior control and social responsibility." *American Psychologist* (1962), *17*, 199-204.

————"Studies of the conditioning of verbal behavior." *Psychological Bulletin* (1958), *55*, 148-70.

————."The therapist as a social reinforcement machine." In H. H. Strupp and L. Luborsky (eds.), *Research in psychotherapy*. Washington, D.C.: American Psychological Association, 1962.

————."The use of generalized reinforcers in psychotherapy research." *Psychological Reports* (1955), *1*, 19-25.

Krasner, L. and L. P. Ullmann. *Research in behavior modification*. New York: Holt, Rinehart & Winston, Inc., 1965.

Krasner, L., L. P. Ullmann, and D. Fisher. "Changes in performance as related to verbal conditioning of attitudes toward the examiner." *Perceptual Motor Skills* (1964), *19*, 811-16.

Krop, H. "Modification of hyperactive behavior of a brain damaged emotionally disturbed child." *The Training School Bulletin* (1971), *68*, 49-54.

Levine, E. S. and D. W. Naiman. "Seminar of behavior modification methods for psychologists working with the deaf." *American Annals of the Deaf* (1970), *115*, 455-91.

Lindsley, O. R. "Experimental analysis of social reinforcement: Terms and methods." *American Journal of Orthopsychiatric* (1963), *33*, 624-33.

———. *Free-operant conditioning and psychotherapy: Current psychiatric therapies.* New York: Grune & Stratton, Inc., 1963.

———. "Operant conditioning methods applied to research in chronic schizophrenia." *Psychiatric Research Report* (1956), *5*, 118-39.

Logan, D. L. and D. Garner. "Effective behavior modification for reducing chronic soiling." *American Annals of the Deaf* (1971), *116*, 382-84.

Lovibond, S. H. "Intermittent reinforcement in behavior therapy." *Behavior Research and Therapy* (1963), *1*, 127-32.

Lovitt, T. "Behavior and modification: The current scene." *Exceptional Children* (1970), *37*, 85-91.

McClain, W. A. "Modification of aggressive classroom behavior through reinforcement, inhibition and relationship therapy." *The Training School Bulletin* (1969), *65*, 122-25.

Mann, L. "Early example of behavior modification in the classroom." *Journal of Special Education* (1971), *4*, 240-41.

Mattos, R. L. *et al.* "Reinforcement and aversive control in the modification of behavior." *Academic Therapy Quarterly* (1969), *5*, 37-52.

Mednick, M. T. and O. R. Lindsley. "Some clinical correlates of operant behavior." *Journal of Social Psychology* (1958), *57*, 13-16.

Molliver, M. E. "Operant control of vocal behavior in the cat." *Journal of Experimental Analysis of Behavior* (1963), *6*, 197-202.

Nessler, M. E. "Behavior modification: Implications for the school counselor." *Journal of Education* (1971), *153*, 12-17.

Perry, P. E. "Behavior modification and social learning theory: Application in the school." *Journal of Education* (1971), *153*, 18-29.

Quay, H. "The effect of verbal reinforcement on the recall of early memories." *Journal of Abnormal Social Psychology* (1959), *59*, 254-57.

Rhodes, W. C. "Psychological techniques and theory applied to behavior modification." *Exceptional Children* (1962), *28*, 333-38.

Ryan, P. A. "Modification of social behavior in the retarded child." *Education* (1970), *90*, 311-14.

Salzinger, K. and S. Pisoni. "Reinforcement of affect responses of schizophrenics during the clinical interview." *Journal of Abnormal Social Psychology* (1958), *57*, 84-90.

Salzinger, K. and M. B. Waller. "The operant control of vocalization in the dog." *Journal of Experimental Analysis of Behavior* (1962), *5*, 383-89.

Sarason, I. G. "The human reinforcer in verbal behavior research." In L. Krasner and L. P. Ullmann (eds.), *Research in behavior modification.* New York: Holt, Rinehart & Winston, Inc., 1965.

Sarbin, T. R. "Hypnosis as a behavior modification technique. "In L. Krasner and L. P. Ullmann (eds.), *Research in behavior modification.* New York: Holt, Rinehart & Winston, Inc., 1965.

Schroeder, W. W. "The effect of reinforcement counseling and model-reinforcement counseling on information-seeking behavior of high school students." Unpublished Ph.D. diss. Stanford University, 1964.

Sheehan, J. G. "The modification of stuttering through non-reinforcement." *Journal of Abnormal Social Psychology (1951)*, *46*, 51-63.

Skinner, B. F. "Operant Behavior." *American Psychologist* (1963), *18*, 503-15.

————. *Science and human behavior*, New York: The Macmillan Company, 1953.

————. *Walden two*. New York: The Macmillan Company, 1948.

Thorpe, J. G., E. Schmidt, and D. Castell. "A comparison of positive and negative (aversive) conditioning in the treatment of homosexuality." *Behavior Research and Therapy* (1963), *1*, 357-62.

Ullmann, L. P., L. Krasner, and B. Collins. "Modification of behavior through verbal conditioning: Effects in group therapy." *Journal of Abnormal Social Psychology* (1961), *62*, 128-32.

Ullmann, L. P., L. Krasner, and D. M. Gelfand. "Changed content within a reinforced response class." *Psychological Reports* (1963), *12*. 819-29.

Wagner, R. F. and B. P. Guyer. "Maintenance of discipline through increasing children's span of attending by means of a token economy." *Psychology in the School* (1971), *8*, 285-89.

Webb, G. A. "School phobia: Pragmatism in behavioral modification techniques." *Elementary School Guidance and Counseling* (1969), *4*, 71-72.

Wetzel, R. J. "Behavior modification, techniques and the training of teacher's aides." *Psychology in the Schools* (1970), *7*, 325-30.

Whitman, M. and J. Whitman. "Behavior modification in the classroom." *Psychology in the Schools* (1971), *8*, 176-86.

Winett, R. A. *et al.* "Child-monitored token reading program." *Psychology in the Schools* (1971), *8*, 259-62.

8

A Token Economy Implemented with Educable Mentally Retarded Pupils

Research has shown that token reinforcement is a powerful tool that can be utilized to enhance academic achievement and appropriate classroom conduct (Bijou, Birnbrauer, Kidder, and Tague, 1966; Broden, Hall, Dunlap, and Clark, 1970). Despite ample evidence to support the effectiveness of token reinforcement procedures, there is a scarcity of literature which focuses on the characteristics of token systems. The purpose of this chapter is to describe a token economy implemented in a special education classroom for educable mentally retarded (EMR) children and offer suggestions for teachers interested in establishing such programs.

This program had the following characteristics:

1. Utilization of mainly tangible rather than social reinforcers;
2. Dispensation of tokens on a primarily continuous schedule at first, gradually shifting to an intermittent schedule;

3. Modification of behaviors of all children within the classroom group rather than of selected individuals;
4. Incorporation of a gradual shift of responsibility from a consultant on token systems to the teacher;
5. Adherence to preplanned procedures for the dispensation of tokens (including verbal, material, and physical contact);
6. Reinforcement of a wide variety of predetermined low probability behaviors;
7. Tokens exchangeable for a wide variety of basic reinforcers;
8. Preplanned strategies employed at the occurrence of inappropriate behaviors;
9. The development of recording forms to enhance the efficiency of the program;
10. A series of observations recorded on pupil and teacher behaviors to estimate the progress of the program;
11. Dispensation of a large number of tokens at the beginning of the program to aid the children in the association of appropriate actions with positive rewards, gradually decreasing as this association was acquired;
12. Maintenance of records concerning the cost of the program.

The program developed as a result of two teachers asking supporting personnel for help in controlling inappropriate behaviors in their classrooms. Both teachers were women serving one year internships as part of the requirements for the masters degree in Mental Retardation. One had eleven years of classroom experience while the other was a first year teacher. The supporting personnel consisted of a university supervisor in special education, who served as the coordinator, and two graduate students, one acting as a field consultant and the other as an observer.

The program was carried out in a public day school with an enrollment of 145 educable and 15 trainable retarded students. Two classes within the school served as a setting. Fourteen students were enrolled in one and eleven in the other. The students ranged in chronological age from 9 to 13 years, with an I.Q. range from 58 to 81.

The Program

An initial conference was held with both teachers. General reinforcement principles were discussed, and a time schedule for each phase of the program was presented. The program was divided into four phases.

Phase I

During the two weeks of phase I, the teachers were instructed to conduct their classes according to normal routine. An observer periodically recorded pupil and teacher behaviors on the Personal Record of School Experiences (PROSE). These observations facilitated the choice of behaviors to be modified through the establishment of a token economy.

Concurrent with these observations, the performance of necessary preplanning activities and chores were being done. Relatively inexpensive items (one cent to one dollar) attractive to most intermediate age EMR children were purchased to serve as basic reinforcers. A store, composed of an attractively covered cardboard box and a medium-size table, was assembled. The store provided a place of redemptions for tokens earned. Peabody Language chips were collected to serve as tokens because of their light weight, durability, and ease of handling. A set of rules concerning the dispensation of chips was developed and presented to the teachers. These were:

1. Dispense a large number of chips at first and gradually decrease the number being given (about 75 to 100 chips to each child the first few days).
2. Only reward appropriate (good) behavior.
3. Completely ignore all disruptive or inappropriate behavior.
4. Never argue with or threaten a child.
5. Never give a chip to a child that asks for one.

| | | | | | Class | Room 10 |
| | | | | | Week | Feb. 15-19 |
Name	Mon.	Tues.	Wed.	Thurs.	Fri.	Total
Mary	75	60	65	42	53	295
John	50	25	35	25	30	165
Tom	60	45	45	50	30	230
Alan						
Cindy						

FIGURE 1.   *Daily record of tokens distributed.*

6. Never toss chips; always take the chip to the child, place your hand on his shoulder, and say, for example, "I like the way you are sitting quietly."
7. If a child questions the reason a chip was dispensed to another child, completely ignore him.
8. If a child asks about the time he gets to go to the store, ignore him.
9. Be consistent.

   To account for the number of chips distributed and the items purchased, recording sheets were constructed. The chart shown in Figure 1 was developed to be used as a day-to-day record of each individual child's chips for a particular week. This later aided the teacher in estimating the quantity of merchandise needed for the store each week. The second chart, Figure 2, was developed to record which items the children bought and how many chips were spent on each. This information aided in the choice of merchandise most attractive to these children.

   At the end of phase I, those behaviors that were to be accelerated were designated. They included working quietly in seat, following the teacher's instructions, raising hand before speaking, and being on time.

Phase II

The implementation of the token economy into the classroom setting was initiated at the beginning of phase II. The system was first introduced into

		Class	Room 10	
		From	Feb. 15	
		To		

Name	Item	Quantity	Cost	Date
James	Hershey bar	2	100	Feb.15
Cindy	jacks	1 set	250	Feb.15
Tom	pencil	1	50	Feb.15
Miles	puzzle	1	100	Feb.16
Lynda	notepad	1	100	Feb.16
Alan	shoe polish	1	290	Feb.17
Marsha	pencil	2	100	Feb.17
Joe				
Amy				

FIGURE 2.   *Record of store purchases.*

the classroom of the first-year teacher and later replicated in the class of the more experienced teacher. One of the supporting personnel, acting as a field consultant, explained the system to the children. He wrote on the chalkboard the behaviors that the children would have to exhibit in order to receive chips, showed them the items redeemable for chips, and subsequently began dispensing chips.

Initially, the teacher continued to work in her usual manner. However, after a few hours she began dispensing chips along with the consultant until, within a week, she gained the skill to dispense chips on her own.

As previously noted, an unusually large number of tokens were distributed to the children during the first two days in order to help the children gain a clear understanding of the benefits that could be reaped from displaying the specified appropriate behaviors. Fifty to seventy-five chips were distributed to each child per day during this time. The number of chips was gradually reduced in successive days until approximately twenty-five to thirty chips were being dispensed to each child per day.

All tokens were distributed on an individual basis. The distribution was based on the appropriate actions of an individual child rather than on the actions of the entire group. The only occasion on which one child's actions could affect the acquisition of tokens by another was when the teacher or consultant tried to draw a child behaving inappropriately back into the group. By giving tokens to pupils around him who were acting appropriately, the misbehaving child could see the consequences of his actions, the consequences being, of course, that everyone was receiving tokens but him. This technique, however, had to be applied with caution. A group of children did, on occasion, use a plant (a student who volunteered to misbehave) in order for the surrounding children to be showered with chips. The group then gave the misbehaving child a "share of the take." This hazard had to be considered but generally the tecnhique worked very effectively to bring misbehaving children under control.

Another aspect that was considered in the dispensation of tokens was the means by which they were dispensed. The authors found it very effective to include material contact (giving the tokens), physical contact (putting a hand on the child's shoulder or head), and verbal contact (telling the child why he is being rewarded). This last component, verbal contact, clarified for the child the behaviors he had exhibited for which he was being rewarded as well as enabling the surrounding children to know what was expected of them if they wished to receive tokens. Material or tangible rewards were not always necessary. After a concept of appropriate behavior had been established, just the physical, verbal, or both were rewarding in themselves and strong enough to sustain the behavior. These are commonly referred to as *social* reinforcers. Social reinforcers were effective, however, only after the concept of appropriate behavior had already been established.

During this phase, the redemption of chips took place twice a day the first two days and once a day the last three days of the first week. Redemption only took place twice during the second week — Wednesday morning and Friday afternoon.

The price of items redeemed from the store was in direct relationship to their original monetary cost. Generally, the technique used was to add a zero to the original price. If the item was worth one penny, it cost ten tokens; if it was worth five cents, it cost fifty tokens. For those items contributed at no cost to the program, an estimated price was assigned and the customary zero added.

As expected, there were some cases in which items chosen by the teacher (and/or consultant) were not highly valued by the children. When it was discovered that certain items were not selling, a sale was held. The items placed on sale were reduced to two-thirds to one-half their original prices. With a record of items bought and redeemed being kept, as previously mentioned, the problem of items not selling was basically eliminated at later stages in the program. Items found successful with intermediate EMR students included jacks, lotions, toy cars, puzzles, combs, pencils, pens, note pads, erasers, balls, jewelry, first aid kits, fingernail polish, shoe polish, candy, fruit, and classroom privileges (playing a game for ten minutes, listening to record player five minutes, etc.).

In phase II data continued to be collected as in phase I, in order to record any changes in behavior that might have occurred after tokens were introduced.

Despite the preparation that was done before the initiation of the program there were problems. One example of a typical problem that was encountered during this period was that the children sometimes played with the chips they had earned when they were supposed to be engaging in a specific task. One means employed to eliminate this undesirable behavior was to reward those children who were attending to their assigned activity while completely ignoring those children who were playing with their chips. Another means employed was that of removing the temptation of playing with the tokens by having a specified place to keep them. A rubber band was given to each child to put around his wrist and every time a token (Peabody Language chip) was dispensed, it was clipped on the rubber band. This also reduced the chances of children stealing chips from others.

Phase III

During phase III outside help was gradually withdrawn from the classroom setting. The consultant was present to help the teacher every other day — Monday, Wednesday and Friday. As a result the teacher was required to take on more responsibility for carrying on the system.

Most activities were conducted in the same manner employed in the previous stage and some with only slight variation. Token dispensation and data collection continued in the same manner. Social reinforcers were dispensed as before, the only difference being that they were more frequently employed. The store was set up in the same way; however, it was held only once a week, Friday afternoons.

It was at this point that the concept and use of the timer were introduced. The timer, a mechanical device that can be set to ring at any given interval, was gradually introduced to aid the teacher in taking full responsibility for her class by the use of intermittent reinforcement. (It is nearly impossible for one individual to provide continuous reinforcement in a large class.) The teacher set the timer for designated intervals of differing time lengths. When the timer rang, the teacher got up from her work and proceeded to reward those children who displayed appropriate behavior during the preceding time interval.

Phase IV

As was the procedure in phase III, tokens were dispensed intermittently with the use of the timer, redemption of chips only took place at the end of each week, and the observer continued to collect data. The only major difference involved the roles of the teacher and consultant. Phase IV included the complete removal of outside help from the classroom environment. The teacher was required to take total responsibility for the token system in her class. The only aid provided the teacher was availability of consultations on specific problems encountered.

Cost of the Program

Contrary to most cases involving the control of a disruptive classroom, the cost of this program was in dollars and cents rather than in teacher frustrations. It cost approximately twenty-five to fifty cents per child per week.

The acquisition of needed materials and items were sometimes free or purchased at discount prices. The chips used as tokens were collected from several Peabody Language kits within the school system. The store was constructed with literally no expense to the teacher. The box was donated by a local grocer. The brightly colored construction paper used to decorate the box and the table used as a platform for the box were available at the school.

Many items for the store itself were also free. They were contributed by local businesses and concerned individuals. The types of items contributed were pens, pencils, balloons, note pads, personal items (hair tonic, hand creams, etc.), and toys. Rentable materials such as games, record players, and athletic equipment were available in the school setting. Free time to engage in an activity of the student's choice was also provided as an item for sale.

After the initial stages of the program in which many tokens were dispensed, the cost of the program decreased as the number of tokens distributed decreased. It was during the later stages that the lower end of the approximated cost (twenty-five cents per child per week) became the best estimate.

A portion of the money needed to operate the program was allotted by the school itself. An interested community agency also contributed merchandise and money to carry on the program. Surprisingly, the monetary cost of the venture was relatively low when the benefits of the program are considered.

Changes in Pupil and Teacher Behaviors

Instrumentation

The instrument used by the observer was *The Personal Record of School Experiences* (PROSE), developed by Donald M. Medley, Carolyn G. Schluck, and Nancy P. Ames. It was developed under the auspices of the Educational Testing Service, Princeton, New Jersey in December, 1968.

> The PROSE is an observational form listing 148 categories of behavior and providing spaces to indicate which of them were emitted by the child, or someone reacting to the child. The form has spaces on the front side of the page to record the subject's interactions with teacher, other adult, or peers. Spaces are also provided to indicate the teacher's activity, the activity and movement in the classroom, and various ways the child interacts with peers, sex and racial group of peer and teacher, and affect shown of either teacher or child. The behaviors are grouped into 11 numbered items called "words," which, when assembled, describe the experience of the child during an event.
>
> The reverse side of the form contains spaces to indicate: the class activity at the time of observation, the child's position in the group, noise and activity level, affective behavior toward others, kind of activity observed, types of school materials the child was playing with, areas in which he was located, and the teacher's behavior which affected the emotional climate in the room.

A timing device, used with a tape recorder and earplug, emits an audible signal at intervals of about 25 seconds. At the signal the observer records what was happening at that moment. One mark is entered in each of the 11 words. These are recorded as "static conditions;" type of contact and sex-racial group are entered as "signs," and "materials and locations" are checked. After each cycle of five events, the back of the form is marked, with checks entering the spaces describing general conditions present at the time of the cycle. The PROSE record for one cycle in the experience of one pupil is completed (Sherman, 1971, pp. 140-41).

Interrater reliability of two observers was determined by a percentage derived from the formula: number of agreements divided by the number of agreements plus the number of disagreements, multiplied by one hundred. The overall reliability for the total instrument was 0.96. The reliability of the subsections ranged from 0.82 to 0. 98.

Twenty to forty-eight observations were recorded per week occurring randomly throughout each week of the study. The position of the observer constantly varied with the position of the teacher and the child being observed.

The choice of this instrument was based on the wide variety of behaviors that could be recorded by the observer. It provided a means of recording adult-pupil interactions, pupil-pupil interactions, and pupil-material interactions, as well as general classroom environment characteristics. Pupil behaviors are recorded throughout and teacher behaviors are included in certain sections of the instrument. In this way discrete behaviors of both pupils and teachers can be easily identified.

Behavior Changes

Two sets of behaviors were compared for both the teacher and the pupils in the two classes. It was the intent of the authors to find what effect tangibly rewarding specific behaviors — working quietly in seat, following the teacher's instructions, raising hand before speaking, and being on time — had on certain behaviors of the teachers and pupils.

As previously stated, observations occurred throughout the program in order to have an objective measure of behavior change. This aided the authors and the teachers in the selection of behaviors which are not conducive to a learning environment and should be modified and also in the estimation of any changes in behaviors after the program was implemented.

The behaviors examined for the teachers were positive and permissive actions versus negative and control. For the students the behaviors were

TABLE 1.   Behaviors of teachers and pupils.

Percentage positive plus permissive and negative plus control behaviors exhibited by teachers; cooperating and distracted plus disruptive behaviors exhibited by pupils.

Phases of the Program		1		2		3		4	
Weeks of the Program		1	2	3	4	5	6	7	8
Teacher's behavior class one	Positive and permissive	4.8%	1.4%	44.3%	28.3%	46.9%	26.0%	22.3%	45.1%
		3.1%		35.4%		38.2%		33.8%	
	Negative and control	44.1%	42.3%	1.3%	1.7%	0.0%	0.0%	0.9%	1.8%
		43.5%		1.2%		0.0%		1.3%	
Teacher's behavior class two	Positive and permissive	12.5%	6.7%	0.0%	64.7%	17.1%	19.7%	21.7%	54.5%
		10.6%		59.5%		19.7%		33.3%	
	Negative and control	9.4%	20.0%	0.0%	1.4%	6.6%	22.7%	1.7%	0.0%
		12.8%		1.3%		15.2%		1.1%	
Pupils' behavior class one	Cooperating	35.2%	37.2%	95.9%	91.8%	38.4%	46.1%	85.5%	94.5%
		36.2%		93.8%		42.3%		90.0%	
	Distracted and disruptive	54.3%	45.0%	4.1%	7.2%	1.2%	46.1%	10.3%	3.6%
		50.0%		5.7%		24.6%		7.0%	
Pupils' behavior class two	Cooperating	27.9%	24.7%	89.1%	97.3%	88.1%	94.5%	99.2%	95.8%
		26.1%		93.0%		91.4%		97.5%	
	Distracted and disruptive	67.1%	64.7%	9.1%	2.0%	8.9%	5.5%	0.8%	2.5%
		65.9%		5.7%		7.1%		1.7%	

Class One — class in which token economy was first introduced.
Class Two — class in which token economy was later replicated.

cooperating versus distracted and disruptive actions. In the top half of Table 1 the behaviors examined for the teachers are shown. The total number of teacher behaviors[*] occurring each week was set to equal 100 percent since this number varied from week to week. The total number of teacher behaviors per week was then used as a base on which to determine increases or decreases in the behaviors under consideration, specifically positive and permissive versus negative and control. The first two lines beside each teacher show the percentage of all teacher behaviors recorded that were positive and permissive (positive and permissive/total teacher behavior). Line one shows the percentage of positive and permissive

---

[*]Total teacher behaviors include positive, permissive, showing and telling, listening and questioning, doing for the pupil, and control and negative, as recorded on the PROSE.

behaviors for each week of the program, while line two shows the percentage for each phase. The second two lines beside each teacher show the percentage of all teacher behaviors recorded that were negative and control behaviors (negative and control/total teacher behaviors). Line three shows the percentage of negative and control behaviors for each week of the program, while line four shows the percentage for each phase.

Cooperating versus distracted and disruptive behaviors of the students are shown in the bottom half of Table 1. The total number of behaviors* for the pupils per week was set to equal 100 percent, as with the teacher behaviors, and used as a base on which to determine increases and decreases in cooperating versus distracted and disruptive behaviors. The first two lines beside each class of pupils show the percentage of cooperating behaviors to the total number of student behaviors (cooperating/total student behaviors). Line one shows the percentage of cooperating behaviors for each week of the program, while line two shows the percentage for each phase. The second two lines beside each class of pupils show the percentage of distracted and disruptive behaviors to the total number of student behaviors (distracted and disruptive/total student behaviors). Line three shows the percentage of negative and control behaviors for each week of the program; line four, the percentage for each phase.

In Table 1 under phase I (weeks 1 and 2), it can be seen that before the token system was introduced into the classroom both teachers exhibited more negative and control behaviors than positive and permissive behaviors. The pupils exhibited more distracted and disruptive than cooperating behaviors.

During the second phase (weeks 3 and 4), the teachers dramatically increased in positive and permissive behaviors and decreased in negative and control behaviors. The introduction of tokens had a similar effect on the pupils by greatly increasing cooperating behaviors while decreasing distracted and disruptive behaviors.

Since a novelty effect may have caused this change, data were collected the following four weeks to check the reliability of the change. For the teachers and the pupils the change held constant during the third phase (weeks 5 and 6), although the difference was not as dramatic as in phase II. It is interesting to note that during week 6 of the program the distracted and disruptive behaviors of the pupils in class one increased, whereas the negative and control behaviors of the teacher in class two increased. During phase IV the negative and control behaviors of the teacher of class two and the distracted and disruptive behaviors of the

---

*Total number of student behaviors include cooperating, distracted, responding to internal stimuli, working on other activities, and disruptive, as recorded on the PROSE.

pupils of class one again decreased. Also, during the last two weeks the positive and permissive behaviors of the teachers and the cooperating behaviors of the pupils increased.

Conclusion

The program described is only one of many different types of token systems that can be initiated. The teachers felt it was an advantageous venture, and the data substantiated their conclusions. It was the decision of the teachers to carry on the system as a regular part of their classroom procedure.

References

Bijou, S. W., J. S. Birnbrauer, J. D. Kidder, and C. Tague. "Programmed instruction as an approach to teaching of reading, writing, and arithmetic to retarded children." *Psychological Record* (1966), *16*, 505-22.

Broden, M., R. V. Hall, A. Dunlap, and R. Clark. "Effects of teacher attention and a token reinforcement system in a junior high school special education class." *Exceptional Children* (1970), *36*, 341-49.

Medley, D. M., C. G. Schluck, and N. P. Ames. "Recording individual pupil experiences in the classroom: A manual for PROSE recorders." Educational Testing Service, 1968.

Sherman, A. "The relationship of teacher behavior and child behavior of four and five year old black disadvantaged children during distar and during nondistar sessions." Unpublished Ed.D. diss., University of Virginia, 1971.

9

Review and
Last-Minute Advice

In preparation for this book eleven people were involved in implementing token systems in public school classrooms. At the close of the school year a meeting was held to discuss the problems and issues of a token system openly. The meeting was recorded and transcribed. After analyzing the teachers' comments, we found that ten basic topics kept coming up. Although these topics have been mentioned throughout the book, we feel it advisable to recapitulate the major problems and issues in one concluding review section.

Expense

The classroom operating on a token economy costs more than the conventional classroom. While this added expense can be a difficult problem to handle, it is not unsolvable. Some school systems, upon the request of the teacher, will help supply the additional funds needed. Supplementing store items with privileges also aids in cutting expenses. For example, some students will purchase ten minutes of free time to listen to records, listen to the radio, or play a favorite game. Some students enjoy the duties of handing out or taking up papers. Homme (1966) mentioned that his children enjoyed pushing him around the room in a caster chair; they also liked to kick a metal wastepaper basket down a flight of stairs. If scheduling can be arranged, students may purchase extra gym or recess time or early dismissal for lunch. Young children enjoy reviewing old ditto papers. Most students would purchase the right to study together. Free time to read comic books or time to do an art project of the student's choice are sellable activities. For more discussion of the problem, review chapter 4.

Efficiency

Many teachers mentioned the difficulty involved in teaching while simultaneously counting specific student behaviors, handing out chips, and giving verbal praise. Superman or Wonderwoman would have difficulty carrying out these four tasks, but they are essential ingredients for the successful operation of any token system. We have suggested the enlistment of an aide or volunteer to help during the initial stages. If outside help is impossible to secure, then we would suggest you go into the system in a small way. For instance, just try it during math period or reading period or just try it for a few things like inseat behavior or work completion. A bit of encouragement comes when you realize that the four tasks will eventually become a habit just as other frequently used teaching techniques become habits. Note: We have never said it would be easy, but as good behavioral habits develop, it will be less difficult. You must sincerely want more out of your class in the way of motivation, discipline, learning, and so on, or a token system will be more work than it's worth. Regardless of what happens, ultimately it will be up to you to decide if the end justifies the means.

    If you are unsure about how to begin, we would suggest you take your math class and try to accelerate the number of correct problems answered on seatwork. Prepare the math seatwork for each child as you would ordinarily do. During the first five days keep all of the papers, grade them as you ordinarily would do, but keep track of the number of correctly answered problems for each day. Purchase a bag of cookies or hard candy, place the edibles in a glass jar, and display it on your desk. On the sixth day explain to the class that you are going to give the students tokens for completing their math paper correctly. If they get all of the problems correct, they will get fifteen tokens; if they get more than half correct, they will get ten tokens, and if they get less than half but at least try, they will get five tokens. If they wish they can purchase a cookie or piece of candy for the price of ten tokens. Fifteen minutes before the class period is over begin to collect the papers and pay the students for their work, i.e., exchange the tokens for the edibles if they decide to cash them in. If some tokens are left over, tell them that they can be used the next day with the newly earned tokens. You should find that the students will work faster and will answer more problems correctly within the second five days than in the first five days. If a student is consistently making errors you may assume he does not understand the concept being taught and may need review or remediation.

After successfully completing the ten-day initial trial period, feel free to give tokens for other things, such as behaving in their seats, having their pencils ready, or starting immediately on the task. Allow the students a chance to earn additional tokens by placing additional seatwork on a table in the front of the room. When a student has completed his first paper, if he wishes, he can get another, different sheet of seatwork.

Begin to try other types of items other than candy and cookies. Start setting up interest centers and in general expand the program in any way you wish.

Mistakes and consistency

Many times you will feel or know that you have given a token away by mistake. You are faced with the problem of fairness; should you allow the token to go unearned or should you take the token back? For example, a student asks you to give him a token and you give it to him. You then immediately realize that you have reinforced asking-for-chip behavior, and it is highly probable that the rate of asking-for-chips behavior will increase. In this case, anticipate the problem and explain to the class that no tokens can be given out when verbally requested, because "it is against the rules." However, for the sake of discussion, let's say the student caught you off guard. He did something that really deserved to be reinforced, but before you had a chance to give him a token, he asked you for one. You were so excited about what he did that was good, you gave him the token. Then all of a sudden you find he is bringing all of his good deeds to your attention and asking for tokens in return. What now? The easiest way out of this situation is to make up a new rule, e.g., "Tokens cannot be given out when someone asks for them."

It may help if you remember that most students are not out to beat the system or the teacher. They are usually trying to find out how to get more tokens. The token system may be one of the best educational things that has happened to them in a long time. If a crisis arises, you may decide to bring it to their attention and ask them what to do about it. This type of problem solving may be worth the trouble and expense of implementing a token system in any classroom.

To avoid a great deal of guesswork as well as mistakes, strive for consistency. You will find that consistency gives you and the students a sense of security. As you plan your token economy, take time to list specific behaviors you want to accelerate so when these behaviors appear you can recognize them and immediately and consistently encourage them through reinforcement. It is easy to branch out from your basic list of specific behaviors (academic and behavioral) and still maintain your consistency and sanity.

There will be times, however, when you feel you have been absolutely wrong about giving out chips for certain behaviors. The best thing to do is to analyze the situation and try to learn from your mistakes. Next time the situation arises search for the behavior you want to increase and zero in on it; you've been here before, so success is assured. Right? Right!

Student decisions

Several teachers experienced situations where the students wanted to decide how many chips a privilege would be worth, to decide how many chips a duty was worth, or to have a certain number of tokens taken away as a means of disciplinary action. In all of the cases mentioned by the teachers the students were harder on themselves than the teacher would have been. In several instances the students were the ones who felt that tokens should be taken away as a means of punishment; the number to be taken away would be all that the student had earned that day. Although student participation is encouraged, under no circumstances should all of the tokens be taken away from any one child for disciplinary reasons.

As mentioned, it is good to allow the students to make group decisions about the token system. Much can be learned by these group encounters. The system isn't the teacher's alone; it also belongs to the students if they have a say in its administration. However, the teacher should be ready to offer suggestions and sometimes point out the possible consequences of certain decisions. If the cost of a privilege is far too high, students should be reminded of the average number of chips earned per day. The teacher should guide the discussion to aid the students in their thinking and should develop some criteria for setting price values on privileges, duties, and discipline actions.

Value of tokens

The importance of the tokens will sometimes vary with the students' mood; that is to say, teachers have found that some days some students just aren't at all interested in the tokens. This could be a catastrophe if your whole system of classroom management is based on tokens and tokens are totally worthless. You feel as though your last trump card has been played and lost.

To guard against deflation of your tokens be sure to be adding and changing the items and/or privileges that can be purchased with the tokens constantly. It would be difficult to develop one set of pay-off items and privileges so exciting that they remain high probability items for every student every day. Regardless of what you have heard or read, there is no giant candy bar up there in the sky. The desires, needs, and interests of the students change as the year progresses. Consequently, your store items and privileges must change to keep in step with the learning, growing, and developing students. As you become familiar with each student's individual personality, you will pick up clues as to some of the things that might interest him. These clues may be observations of what a student does with his spare time. Sometimes the best clues are answers to some direct questions such as "What are you interested in?" or "What do you like to do?" One teacher mentioned that she found that her most aggressive student was taking judo lessons. She purchased a judo book with a lot of pictures in it, and she found that the student would behave in order to earn tokens which could be used to purchase pages from the book. Since it would take too long for the student to purchase the entire book, the teacher just sold him the pages one by one. New books and new filmstrips pertaining to different interests always add a spark of life to any token system. Rotate games and puzzles frequently, choose new art media at least every two weeks, put certain activities to rest for a month or two and then bring them out again for revitalized life. It will be easy to decide which items or activities are actually not selling by their decreased use. You may find that some areas always remain popular. If you find this happening, don't look a gift horse in the mouth. Consider yourself extremely lucky and don't attempt to tamper with it.

Hold back an ace in the hole: a new game, a new mystery story tape with a surprise ending, or a secret code message with bubble gum for those who decode the message. For depression days when the bottom falls out of the token market, play your aces and then scramble to find new ones. Of course, if you run out of aces, remember that you are no worse off than you were before the token system started.

Students' use of the system for their own ends

There will most certainly be times when you notice the students are turning the tables on you. They will leave their seats so that they will be given a token for returning to their seats. Of if a student receives a token for asking to sharpen his pencil, the entire class may see a need to sharpen pencils. These events really aren't as bad as they may sound. The students are demonstrating they want your praise and tokens so they will follow your lead. Remember, you're in the driver's seat. When you find yourself in this situation, quickly find the behavior you want and reinforce it. There will always be someone working on an assignment or reading a book or getting ready to study. Give these behaviors your full attention and praise.

Teachers often encourage children to raise their hands to signal when they want to try to answer a question or when they want the teacher's attention. A complaint was made by one teacher that after the hand was raised and the token was given to the student, the student returned to his never-never-land, daydreaming. The teacher reinforced hand raising, but she really wanted the student to raise his hand and attend to what was going on in class. As the teacher, you can reinforce more than one thing. You can be selective and reinforce only those who are raising their hands and listening as long as you are verbally specific about the behaviors for which the tokens are being provided. Always be specific about what behavior you want. Don't make a guessing game out of the system. Too many children get turned off because they don't know what is expected of them. Learning to behave is like learning to read: those who break the code become excited and enjoy it; those who do not are left on the outside and drop out.

Token economy cannot stand alone

A token economy is an effective and powerful learning tool but it is misused when it is used in place of curriculum. Teachers must continue to plan interesting and challenging assignments, prepare adequate seatwork, organize interesting presentations, and develop exciting activities and interest centers. These are all factors that are necessary in any good classroom. They are no less important in a classroom using a token economy.

Saving tokens

Some teachers expressed concern about teaching the concept of saving tokens. Whether or not you teach saving is an individual preference. It would be difficult to establish guidelines that would be applicable for all teachers in all situations. However, the concept of saving tokens is closely related to teaching students to delay gratification and therefore is extremely important to the successful operation of any token economy.

During the initial stages it is important that the students learn how to exchange the tokens for desirable things and begin to view the tokens as representing good things. This association is first developed by allowing the tokens to be exchanged quickly. Later it is desirable to hold store only once a week. This delay is one means of teaching a child to delay gratification and is also a step toward teaching a child to save or at least hold his tokens until store time. Most students learn very quickly to save tokens in order to purchase more expensive items. Many students learn the concept of saving but when store time arrives find it difficult to keep from buying inexpensive things even though they want the more expensive items. Some students have difficulty understanding what ten tokens versus fifty tokens versus 100 tokens will buy. One teacher taught a child to understand the concept of 100. An item was found that the child said he wanted. The item was immediately priced at 100 tokens. It was placed in the store "on reserve" for the child. The teacher made a grid of 100 squares on a piece of 8 1/2″ x 11″ paper (ten squares across and ten squares down). At the end of the first day the child counted his tokens. For each token a square was crossed out. At the completion of day one the child ended up with thirty-eight tokens — thirty-eight squares were crossed out. He was shown that he needed sixty-two more tokens to buy the coveted item in the store. At the end of day two he added thirty-two to the thirty-eight and was shown that he needed thirty more tokens. On day three he purchased the item. Most students learn this concept on their own with little help; but if a child has some difficulty catching on to the numerical system, a direct approach may be used to facilitate learning.

In some cases the child understands the numerical concepts but just can't save for the thing he says he wants. In cases such as these, the items may be rented or possibly parts of the items may be purchased rather than saving for the whole thing. For example, a child in one class wanted a model car to build but just couldn't seem to save enough tokens to purchase the model kit. As a compromise the pieces of the model were sold separately. At the end of day one, for instance, he might purchase the wheels to the car or the engine or the glue. In a somewhat elaborate system it was reported that a bicycle was purchased in this manner and was actually built in a corner of the room.

Although saving may be considered a value-related concept and thus not encouraged by some teachers, there is something to say about the importance of teaching the concept of saving. After the concept has been learned you can leave it up to the individual child whether to save or not to save.

Arguing and rebellious students

The token system should minimize arguing and rebellious behavior. But what do you do if these situations arise? Remember, it takes two parties to argue. You, as the teacher, can simply refuse to argue with the student. You can also refer the disagreement to the whole class for discussion. We have mentioned this type of group process earlier. If you find yourself getting upset, you may try discussing the matter with the student later on in private, when you both are a bit calmer. With openly hostile and rebellious behavior it is of the utmost importance for the teacher to remain calm. Keep calm. Keep your voice low and steady, because some students demonstrate defiant behaviors just to see the teacher get upset. Use your tokens to reinforce those students who maintain proper behavior in the face of rebellion. If you can preserve control over the majority of the class members, you can probably outlive the rebellious ones. His persistence may cost the rebellious student a good number of tokens. Your calm persistence is much more effective and lasting than negative verbal encounters or physical punishment directed to the rebel. There is no disgrace in letting those who are behaving properly know that you appreciate and need their support. This reinforcement will many times aid in the development of strong positive class relationships. We must reiterate, much planning and forethought of assignments, seatwork, presentation, and activities are the best accompaniments to the token economy and will assist in the constriction of insolent behavior.

Moral issues

The basic moral issue brought up by the token economy seems to focus on the question of who has the right to manipulate another individual or who has the right to impose his values on another. The easiest way for us to handle this issue is to state directly that if a teacher questions his right to set academic or behavioral goals for children, and furthermore questions the use of directive techniques to obtain these goals, it is highly probable that this teacher would be more successful in using something other than a token economy in his classroom. However, confronting the moral question in this manner may in fact be skirting the issue.

Some people view the behaviorist on a continuum, diametrically opposed to the humanist. The humanist is defined as the warm, sensitive individual who assists children in their development through a nurturing process that develops self-worth, self-image, and self-esteem. They believe that as children find their true selves they begin to grow. Much, if not all, of the learning is directed by the child rather than the teacher. The behaviorist, on the other hand, is looked on as a technician who sets goals for the learner and assists the learner in obtaining these goals through environmental manipulation, *i.e.,* controlling various stimuli and reinforcers. By using these definitions, it is theoretically possible to have a humanist that is warm, sensitive, and views the learner as the center of learning at one extreme of the continuum while at the other extreme have the behaviorist as a distant technician who views the learner as being almost incapable of learning without the careful manipulation of the environment. Although most teachers operate somewhere between the two extremes, the dichotomy is helpful in exploring the question of who has the right to manipulate another person. Most behaviorists really aren't concerned about the question because they see all learning as being one person manipulating the environmental events of another person. In other words, one person (teacher) manipulates the environment of the other (child) to change the behavior of the other. This is the process of education. Remember, we said in the first chapter that effective education changes kids; effective teachers change kids; the worst thing that could happen to a teacher would be to expose his talents and skills to a child and have the child remain unaffected. The humanist is the individual most bothered by the question. Since, according to the humanist, most meaningful learning comes from inside the learner, the manipulation of environmental events is considered an imposition on the learner. Humanists realize that people can be manipulated but think that this manipulation is not honorable. Yet, as you study the goal for which a humanist strives, self-actualization, the question of manipulation becomes answerable within the humanist framework. As a learner grows and develops the goal is to become himself, his real self, to be a self-actualized person. A self-actualized person is a person who is sensitive; experiences fully, vividly, and totally; indulges in self inquiry; knows himself; is honest; is self-aware; and has many peak experiences. In short, this person is a man among men. This person knows himself as well as his fellow man.

According to Maslow (1971) the self-actualized individual is a most healthy person and is "ought-perceptive," i.e., he seems to be less "ought-blind." He seems to understand situations and is capable of making value decisions. Maslow poses the question:

> If we want to answer the question how tall can the human species grow, then obviously it is well to pick out the ones who are already tallest and study them. If we want to know how fast a human being can run, then it is no use to average out the speed of a "good sample" of the population; it is far better to collect Olympic gold medal winners and see how well they can do. If we want to know the possibilities for spiritual growth, value growth, or moral development in human beings, then I maintain that we can learn most by studying our most moral, ethical, or saintly people (p. 7).

This line of reasoning seems to be apropos to the question of who has the right to manipulate other people. Ironically the humanists (the people most bothered by the question) may have the best answer. The answer is the self-actualized individual. The next question is whether a self-actualized individual would use a token economy in the best interests of his fellow man. As with most theoretical issues, this issue produces more questions than answers. Yet, one point should be clear; that is, the teacher using a token system must be aware of his power; he must be sensitive to the children's needs, be humane, and possess some good old horse sense; he should be self-actualized himself.

Something to
Think About

We are unsure about the best approach to closing this book. We could give you a pep talk in an attempt to psyche you up for the big moment; however, we have chosen just to talk with you about some of our personal concerns about a token system. We have mentioned several times that implementing a token system is very hard work. There is nothing magical about the tokens, but when they become reinforcing the children will probably become strongly motivated and begin turning out much more work than they have completed in the past. It is not unusual for a motivated child to complete three to four times the amount of academic work under a token system than he was completing under traditional instruction. This means more work for the teacher in preparing material for the motivated child. Principals have remarked that they can immediately tell when a teacher begins a token system in his classroom because he uses three times the amount of paper he used to use, and he spends more time running the ditto machine.

We have witnessed teachers instructing children to copy sentences off of the board, who after beginning a token system, find that students copy so fast the teacher can't keep them busy. Some teachers become so concerned about this that they misuse the system. Instead of having the students copy the material once, they have the students copy the same material ten or even up to twenty times or more. This is a gross misuse of the system and is unfair to the students, the system, and the school. Some teachers used to consider themselves lucky when the majority of the students completed one ditto sheet of math problems during math period. Then suddenly after beginning a token system they found that the dittoed sheet could be completed in five or ten minutes. Confrontation with the idle kids forces a teacher to resort to more dittos, many of which are nothing but busy work. This is also a misuse of the system, yet we have observed it happen again and again. After analyzing some of these unfortunate cases, we think the system was misused because of two main reasons: surprise and confusion, and gravity and solemnity.

Surprise and confusion

One reason the system may be misused is because the teacher is surprised to see children get excited about school so quickly and run out of work to do. These teachers know the danger of having idle students in a classroom. As teacher anxiety goes up, confusion sets in. As a result dittos are churned out by the ream or students are required to copy things over again and again. This may later be justified verbally by "They need the practice" or "There's value in repetition." These statements may be true, but there comes a time when too much repetition becomes a misuse of the system. A feasible substitute for repetition may be interest centers where the children can work quietly after completing their individual work, or games such as checkers, Candyland, old maid, or jacks, which the children can play after completing their work. These interest centers and activities can also be purchased with tokens earned for work completion or good behavior. Not only is it next to impossible to make each minute academically exciting and challenging for each student, it may not be entirely academically healthy. We are not advocating all fun and games, but we also are not advocating all work and no play.

Gravity and solemnity

Possibly one of the main reasons token systems fail is because teachers take themselves too seriously. They get so worked up about education and about the token system they forget to take it easy and have a little fun. Granted, the system is a lot of work but it should be a lot of fun too. It should be fun to see kids race through their work. It is fun to see kids horde or save tokens for certain items. It's fun to see tokens burn a hole in a student's pocket. It's fun to listen to kids talk about what they are going to do with their tokens. It's fun to see students try to outmaneuver adults. Sometimes it's fun to be outmaneuvered.

There is a grave danger when people begin to take themselves too seriously and you must constantly be on the lookout for solemnity setting in. Townsend (1970) mentions that "Billy Graham has a man named Grady Wilson who yells Horseshit — however you say that in Baptist — at him whenever he takes himself too seriously" (p. 85). Most teachers don't have a Grady Wilson around, but maybe your principal or supervisor might fill in in a pinch.

In one class, getting a drink of water became a problem, so the teacher started charging a token for each drink. Suddenly getting a drink became sort of a status thing; all of the kids in the class wanted to get a drink; in fact, one day, the water fountain was in use all day. The price for drinks went up, but the children continued to pay inflated prices for drinks of water. The constant drinking got on the teacher's nerves, so she explained to the students that the constant drinking bothered her. As a result getting a drink of water was restricted to only certain periods of the day. The drinking period rule was accepted immediately by everyone. Later a student got the idea that he would start his own business and asked permission to set up a kool-aid stand. Talk about making education relevant — the kool-aid stand led to the development of a cookie stand, a bank, a house of chance, a secret club, taxes on desks, the election of a class commissioner, etc. The class actually developed into a self-contained community.

All classes should have their fun moments. It is up to you to see to it that learning is fun. Please don't misunderstand: some learning is far from fun, but through the use of a token system, this distasteful but necessary learning can be accomplished as quickly as possible so fun times can happen and can be enjoyed.

In closing, if after two weeks of honestly trying to implement a token system in your classroom, you find it more work than fun, we would strongly urge you to discontinue the system. As we have said before, this system is not for everyone. Give it a two-weeks trial period and you will know if it is for you. If you try it you may just like it. Good luck!!

The Stainbacks and the Paynes

References

Homme, L. E. "Human motivation and encouragement." *The University of Kansas symposium, The learning environment: Relationship to behavior modification and implications for special education* (1966), *16*, 30-39.

Maslow, A. H. *The farther reaches of human nature.* New York: The Viking Press, 1971.

Townsend, R. *Up the organization.* New York: Alfred A. Knopf, Inc., 1970.